Introduction

The successful use of helicopters armed with machine-guns and rocket launchers by the US Army during the Vietnam War gave rise to a new class of combat aircraft, namely gunship helicopters. Several nations began developing helicopters intended for destroying enemy personnel and ground vehicles (including armoured ones) as a complement to fixed-wing attack aircraft. The Soviet Union did not miss this trend either; the first attempts to create an attack helicopter dated back to the early 1950s when the Mil' Mi-1 (NATO reporting name *Hare*) was equipped with anti-tank guided missiles, but this version saw only limited use with the Soviet Air Force.

In Poland, which was entrusted with licence production of the Mil' Mi-2 *Hoplite* light utility helicopter for all customers, a number of armed versions were developed (the Mi-2PPK, Mi-2URN and the like); these saw service with the air arms of Poland, East Germany and a few other countries but failed to attract interest on the part of the Soviet military. On the other hand, the eminently successful Mi-8 *Hip* medium utility helicopter had several mass-produced armed versions and saw action in numerous conflicts, including the Afghan War. It also paved the way for the Mi-24 combat helicopter described here – the first of the kind in the Soviet Union. In turn, the positive experience with the Mi-24 triggered the development of other helicopters tailored for combating enemy ground forces in situations when using fast jets is inexpedient and providing close air support to friendly ground forces.

This book deals with the principal attack helicopters of the present-day Russian Army. It will be of interest not only to readers with an interest in military history but also to scale modellers; the book gives an overview of the plastic kits of the helicopters described here and includes line drawings and colour schemes that will help modellers choose the best kit and build a good and correctly painted model.

Above: Aptly coded '52 Yellow', a pre-production Ka-52 powers up before a flight.

Left: '29 Yellow', an updated Mi-24PN sporting a rather faded camouflage scheme.

Acknowledgements
This book is illustrated by photos by: Yefim Gordon, Andrey Zinchuk, Dmitriy Pichugin, Viktor Drushlyakov, Aleksandr Bel'tyukov, Sergey Ryabtsev, Mikhail Gribovskiy, as well as photos from the archives of the Mil' Moscow Helicopter Plant, the Kamov Company, Rostvertol and Yefim Gordon. Colour artwork: Andrey Yurgenson, Viktor Mil'yachenko, Mikhail Bykov, Sergey Ignat'yev. Line drawings: Mil' Moscow Helicopter Plant, Kamov Company. The authors have referred to the following sources: www.aircraftresourcecenter.com, www.anhelix.narod.ru, www.arcair.com, www.cybermodeler.com, www.fanakit.free.fr, www.heliborne.ru, www.helikits.net, www.helmo.gr, www.hobby.dn.ua, www.ivan.brocot.free.fr, www.karopka.ru, www.kits.kitreview.com, www.km.ru, www.maximodelizm.com.ua, www.militaryrussia.ru, www.model-making.eu, www.modelingmadness.com, www.modellversium.de, www.modelkitworkshop.blogspot.ru, www.scalemodels.ru, www.sdelanounas.ru, www.1001modelkits.com.

Mil' Mi-24

The 'Flying Crocodile'

As early as 1958 the Moscow-based OKB-329 design bureau led by General Designer Mikhail L. Mil' (*opytno-konstrooktorskoye byuro* – experimental design bureau) began development of an armed assault/transport version of the Mi-4 *Hound* piston-engined medium helicopter. Initially the Soviet military failed to show interest; it was not until 1965 that the Mi-4AV was fielded. When the Mi-4's successor, the twin-turboshaft Mi-8, was developed and built in the early 1960s, Mikhail L. Mil' floated the idea of developing a dedicated troopship/assault helicopter which would be a kind of airborne counterpart of the BMP infantry fighting vehicle (IFV).

In 1966 the OKB's prototype construction facility built a full-size mock-up of such a helicopter which bore the in-house designation **V-24** (V stood for *vertolyot* – helicopter). Despite having almost nothing in common with the actual Mi-24 prototype that appeared several years later (in fact, the mock-up looked like a Bell UH-1 Huey with stub wings added), it incorporated the principal features of the future assault helicopter: a crew of two – a pilot and a weapons systems operator (WSO), a troop/cargo cabin big enough to accommodate eight troops with full kit, and heavy armament. The latter comprised a 23-mm (.90 calibre) cannon, four to six anti-tank guided missiles (ATGMs) or two to four rocket pods, each holding sixteen 57-mm (2.24-in) S-5 folding-fin aircraft rockets (FFARs). The cockpit, troop cabin and vital systems had armour protection.

Mil' submitted his 'flying IFV' concept to the command of the Soviet Armed Forces. He found supporters among the younger military theoreticians, but he had his share of opponents as well; these were mainly high-ranking Ministry of Defence officials headed by the then-Minister of Defence, Marshal of the Soviet Union Rodion Ya. Malinovskiy, who preferred more traditional weapons systems to helicopters. In 1967 Mil' persuaded the Minister's First Deputy, Marshal of the Soviet Union Andrey A. Grechko who had always favoured combat helicopters, to form a special expert panel and look more deeply into the matter. The opinions of military experts ranged from open support to blunt rejection, but the supporters won and Mil' received the go-ahead. On 29th March 1967 the USSR Council of Ministers' Presidium's Commission on Defence Industry Matters issued a ruling ordering the Mil' OKB to prepare and submit a project of a battlefield support helicopter. Two preliminary design projects were prepared in short order – a 7-tonne (15,430-lb) helicopter with a single Izotov TV3-117 turboshaft engine and a 10.5-tonne (23,150-lb) helicopter powered by two TV3-117s. The military approved the twin-engine version but specified that the helicopter be armed with a fast-firing heavy machine-gun and the Shtoorm (Assault) supersonic ATGMs then under development. The helicopter was to have a weapons control system comprising a stabilised sight for the WSO, a computing sight for the pilot and a laser rangefinder. Night-capable targeting systems and defensive avionics were to be incorporated as they became available.

The Mi-24 programme was officially launched by a joint Communist Party Central Committee/Council of Ministers directive issued on 6th May 1968. Work on the advanced development project began immediately under the overall supervision of Mikhail L. Mil' (succeeded after his death in 1970 by Marat N. Tishchenko). The design effort was led by Deputy Chief Designer V. A. Kuznetsov.

The V-24, also known by the in-house product code *izdeliye* (product) 240, utilised a conventional single-rotor layout with a five-blade main rotor and a three-blade tail rotor. The slender fuselage was very clean aerodynamically. The crew sat in tandem under a common angular canopy, with the pilot behind and to the left of the WSO. The latter detected and identified targets, fired the ATGMs, worked the flexible machine-gun in the nose and dropped bombs. The pilot could fire the rockets or podded guns on the wing stations and the machine-gun, providing the latter was aligned and fixed in the direction of flight. Later, in service, the crew of the Mi-24 was increased to three by adding a flight engineer. The centre fuselage was occupied by a troop/cargo cabin accommodating up to eight troopers back to back, with the engines and the main gearbox above it. The cabin had horizontally split doors on both sides (the upper and lower halves of each door opened simultaneously by means of mechanical linkages and the lower half incorporated boarding steps); the cabin windows could be opened, allowing the troopers to use their assault rifles in flight. Further aft the fuselage blended into a tapered tailboom terminating in a fairly large tail rotor pylon with an asymmetrical airfoil to offload the tail rotor in forward flight.

A distinctive feature of the V-24 was the small stub wings with zero dihedral and strong incidence located aft of the cabin; the wings not only carried the weapon pylons but reduced rotor disc loading in forward flight by 19-25%. Another novel feature was the retractable tricycle undercarriage, the main units stowing in bays aft of the cabin and the nose unit under the cockpit floor.

To speed up development the General Designer took the decision to use, inasmuch as possible, the dynamic components from the Mi-8's naval amphibious derivative, the Mi-14 *Haze* – the powerplant, rotor system and parts of the power train. The new TV3-117 turboshaft designed for the Mi-14 by the Leningrad-based OKB-117 under General Designer Sergey P. Izotov was then one of the best helicopter engines, on a par with foreign engine types. If one engine failed, the other automatically went from 1,700-shp nominal power to 2,200-shp take-off/contingency rating. The main rotor shaft (and the whole powerplant package) was inclined 2.5° to starboard relative to the vertical plane. This made it possible to significantly reduce the V-24's bank and side-slip in straight and level flight (phenomena which are inevitable for all single-rotor helicopters); thereby the weapons aiming and firing accuracy could be appreciably enhanced.

Left and below: A mock-up of the very first V-24 project looking remarkably like the Bell UH-1 with stub wings. Note the horizontally split cabin doors, the twin-barrel cannon on the starboard skid and the odd 'shoot the sky' angle of the 9M17M Falanga ATGMs (apparently no one had considered the wing incidence).

Much attention was given to survivability and crew protection. The cockpit and cabin formed a single pressurised cell with a slight pressure differential being maintained to prevent ingress of radioactive dust, chemical or biological agents when operating in an NBC environment. The cockpit had a bullet-proof windscreen and an armoured pilot's seat; the cockpit and cabin sides were armour-plated, as were the engine cowlings. The cabin could also accommodate casualties on stretchers or up to 1,500 kg (3,310 lb) of cargo. Outsize loads weighing up to 2,000 kg (4,410 lb) could be carried externally slung.

Detail design work commenced in August 1968. In February 1969 the government commission reviewed and accepted the project and the full-scale mock-up. The first prototype was completed in June that year.

The intended weapons fit was not yet ready by the time the first V-24 was completed; therefore a decision was taken to equip the helicopter with the K-4V weapons system which had achieved a good service record on the Mi-4AV. Two detachable cantilever racks were mounted low on the centre fuselage sides, each carrying two launch rails for 9M17M *Falanga-M* (Solifuge-M; NATO code name AT-2 *Swatter*) ATGMs. The WSO guided the missiles manually, using radio control. A 12.7-mm (.50 calibre) Afanas'yev A-12.7 heavy machine-gun on an NUV-1 gimballed mount was installed in the nose; it was aimed by means of a PKV collimator gunsight. The wing pylons could carry UB-32 rocket pods (each holding thirty-two S-5 FFARs), four bombs of 100-/250-kg (221-/551-lb) calibre or two 500-kg (1,102-lb) bombs or napalm tanks.

The manufacturer's tests of the V-24 (Mi-24) began on 15th September 1969 with tethered flights. Four days later test pilot Gherman V. Alfyorov performed the first free flight. Shortly thereafter the second prototype was built; it was followed by a test batch of ten helicopters – five manufactured by the OKB's prototype construction facility near Moscow (plant No. 329) and five by aircraft factory No. 116 in Arsen'yev, in the Soviet Far East (later known as AAPO ***Progress*** – the 'Progress' Arsen'yev Aircraft Production Association). The greater part of the manufacturer's test programme was conducted on these machines. One of the Arsen'yev-built helicopters was completed as a weapons testbed for the Shtoorm-V ATGM. Apart from Alfyorov, test pilots Gurghen R. Karapetian, Marat A. Material'nyy and others took part in the test flights. Actually the *izdeliye* 240 prototype version with zero-dihedral wings was the *second* to become known in the West, hence its NATO reporting name *Hind-B*.

State acceptance (i.e., certification) trials began in June 1970, proceeding intensively for the next 18 months. They generally confirmed the designers' expectations. Despite a considerable increase in cruising speed compared to the Mi-8, the V-24's vibration levels turned out to be relatively low. However, the pilots encountered a number of problems which necessitated substantial changes to the helicopter's design. At speeds in excess of 200 km/h (124 mph) with the autopilot disengaged, the helicopter was prone to pitch and roll oscillations (known as Dutch roll) that persisted or subsided only slowly; these oscillations provoked by outside disturbances required the pilot to make corrective actions all the time. To improve lateral stability, the stub wings were

The unmarked first prototype V-24 at a military hardware display for the Soviet government. Note the zero-dihedral wings with four UB-32A FFAR pods and the launchers for Falanga ATGMs ahead of them.

This aspect of the V-24 prototype (with markings added) during trials shows clearly the cantilever racks carrying the ATGM launch rails. Here, dummy bombs are suspended under the wings. Note the two portside cockpit doors.

redesigned, gaining substantial anhedral (12°). Immediately, another problem arose: the ATGMs carried on the fuselage sides could be struck by the rockets leaving the underwing pods; besides, the launchers were located in line with the cabin doors, rendering the latter unusable. Therefore the fuselage-mounted launchers were abandoned in favour of vertical wing endplates with transverse bars carrying the missile rails; thus the V-24 acquired its signature drooped wings with downturned wingtips.

Mock-up studies showed that the first V-24s had not enough room to accommodate the envisaged fast-firing machine-gun and ***Ra**duga-F* (Rainbow-F) guidance system for the improved 9M17P Falanga-PV ATGMs (the F suffix was a reference to the Falanga missiles). To cure the problem a slightly longer cockpit section was introduced. Besides, at the demand of the military the WSO's station was provided with rudimentary flight controls, allowing him to take over if the pilot was wounded and bring the chopper home. However, because of delays in the development of the intended armament the helicopter entered production at the Arsen'yev plant in 1970 with the old Falanga-M missile system and the A-12.7 machine-gun; in this guise it was known as the **Mi-24A** (*izdeliye* 245). Deliveries to Soviet Air Force units began in 1971. A year later, upon completion of the State acceptance trials, the Mi-24A was officially included into the inventory. The NATO reporting name was *Hind-A*.

Early-production Mi-24As had the tail rotor on the starboard side, as on the Mi-8; however, the helicopter had poor directional control in some flight modes, and service pilots were quick to point this out. Therefore in 1972 the tail rotor was relocated to port, switching from pusher to tractor configuration (as on the Mi-14 and Mi-8MT/Mi-17 *Hip-H*) so that the forward blade went against the main rotor downwash; this increased tail rotor efficiency dramatically. The new design was introduced on production *Hind-As* in 1973. In 1970-74 the Arsen'yev plant built more than 240 Mi-24A helicopters.

A trainer version designated **Mi-24U** (*oo**cheb**nyy* – training, used attributively), or *izdeliye* 244, was tested in 1972 and built in small numbers. It lacked the nose-mounted machine-gun and provisions to carry ATGMs; the instructor occupied the former WSO's position which featured flight instrumentation and full flight controls. The Mi-24U was code-named *Hind-C*.

Concurrently with the introduction of the Mi-24A into service the Mil' OKB continued to perfect its armament on a development aircraft designated **Mi-24B** (*izdeliye* 241). It differed from the Mi-24A in featuring a USPU-24 powered nose barbette which mounted a Yakushev/Borzov YakB-12.7 four-barrel Gatling machine-gun; this was slaved to a KPS-53AV sighting system which automatically made corrections for the helicopter's movement during firing. The system included an analogue computer working in conjunction with an air data system. Also, the Mi-24B was armed with Falanga-PV ATGMs having semi-automatic command line-of-sight (SACLOS) guidance, which increased 'kill' probability three to four times. The Raduga-F guidance system featured gyrostabilised low light-level television (LLLTV) and forward-looking infra-red (FLIR) sensors and enabled the helicopter to make evasive manoeuvres while firing the missiles, thereby considerably enhancing combat survivability.

This page:
'77 Red', the prototype of the Mi-24A, showing the anhedral wings with vertical endplates carrying the ATGM launch rails and the A-12,7 machine-gun in the nose. Note also the longer cockpit section.

The early-production Mi-24As with starboard-side tail rotors.

Mi-24As support a unit of T-55 main battle tanks during a Soviet Army exercise. Note that the wingman's helicopter is a late example with a portside tail rotor.

A pair of late-production Mi-24As with portside tail rotors.

Right: This late Mi-24A is preserved in the museum of the Aviakon repair plant in Konotop, the Ukraine.

Below: The full-size mock-up of the Mi-24B, showing the USPU-24 nose barbette with a YakB-12,7 machine-gun and the excrescence of the Raduga-F targeting/guidance system sensor pack. Note the V-24 style short nose, zero-dihedral wings and low-set ATGM launcher racks.

Bottom: One of the actual Mi-24B development aircraft converted from an early Mi-24A.

The Mi-24B successfully passed initial trials in 1971-72, but further development was discontinued. The reason was the Mi-24A's major weakness – the horizontally staggered seating of the crew created large 'blind spots', and the 'greenhouse' canopy with flat glazing panels created annoying reflections. Therefore, back in early 1971 the Mil' OKB undertook a radical redesign: the forward fuselage was more streamlined, the pilot and WSO being accommodated in individual vertically-staggered tandem cockpits. The narrow cockpits had extensive armour protection and bubble canopies with optically-flat bulletproof windscreens giving far better all-round visibility. Again, the USPU-24 barbette was incorporated. The redesign also afforded a wider field of view for the sensors and guidance antenna of the Raduga-F

The first prototype Mi-24D (note the starboard-side tail rotor). The stepped-tandem cockpits with individual canopies are clearly visible.

system, but this required the nose gear unit to be lengthened to ensure adequate ground clearance for the LLLTV/FLIR sensor fairing, giving the helicopter a pronounced nose-up attitude on the ground. 'Wet' wing pylons were introduced, permitting carriage of 500-litre (110 Imp. gal) drop tanks and leaving the cabin free on long-range missions.

Unfortunately the intended Shtoorm-V (*vertolyotnyy* – heliborne) missiles were still unavailable, and the version allocated the designation Mi-24V (next in the Cyrillic alphabetical sequence after the Mi-24B; see below) was put on hold. As the next-best thing, the Mil' OKB developed a combination of the new airframe with the old armament based on the 9M17P missiles. This interim version was designated **Mi-24D** or *izdeliye* 246 (the designation Mi-24G, which would have been next in the sequence, was skipped). The two prototypes were converted in June 1972 from early-production Mi-24As and thus were unique in having a starboard-side tail rotor. State acceptance trials began the next year, continuing well into 1974, and the helicopter passed them with flying colours. Also in 1973, the Mi-24D entered production at AAPO Progress and the Rostov Helicopter Production Association (plant No. 168, now known as Rostvertol).

An export version with slightly downgraded mission avionics designated **Mi-25** was developed for the Soviet Union's Warsaw Pact allies and friendly Third World countries. The Mi-24D/Mi-25's NATO reporting name was *Hind-D*. A trainer version designated **Mi-24DU** (*izdeliye* 249) appeared in 1980, differing from the standard Mi-24D in

Another Mi-24D prototype with the tail rotor on the port side.

An armourer removes the safety pins from the fuses of FAB-250 bombs hooked up to an operational Mi-24D.

lacking the USPU-24 gun barbette and having dual controls (the launch rails and associated guidance equipment for the Falanga-P missiles were retained). The export version of the Mi-24DU was designated **Mi-25U**. More than 620 *Hind-Ds* had been built when production ended in 1983.

The 9K113 Shtoorm-V weapons system based on the 9M114 (AT-6 *Spiral*) tube-launched supersonic ATGM was finally submitted for trials in 1972, and the **Mi-24V** (*izdeliye* 242) was born. In comparison with the Falanga-PV the new missile offered higher speed, longer range and greater accuracy; besides, it was more compact. Again, the missile had SACLOS guidance, and the suitably modified targeting/guidance system was designated Raduga-Sh, the suffix letter referring to the Shtoorm missile. The disposable launch tubes were attached by quick-release fittings to the vertical wing endplates. Trials of the 9K113 weapons system were completed in 1974. Normally two or four missiles were carried on the endplate stations, although the Mi-24V is known to have carried as many as 16 (!) Shtoorm ATGMs during trials, using the wing pylons and special adapters.

Apart from the missiles, the Mi-24V differed in having TV3-117V engines (*vysotnyy* – with improved altitude performance) uprated to 2,225 shp for hot-and-high conditions; they retained the 1,700-shp nominal rating up to the altitude of 1,000 m (3,280 ft) at ambient temperatures of 40°C (104°F), whereas the TV3-117 gave only 1,420 shp in similar conditions). New communications equipment was fitted (an R-863 VHF radio and an R-828 radio for communication with ground troops), an ASP-17V computing gunsight was provided for the pilot, and the SRO-2M Khrom (Chromium; NATO *Odd Rods*) identification friend-or-foe transponder was replaced by the new SRO-1P *Parol'* (Password).

The Mi-24V prototype was converted from an early-production Mi-24D in 1973. State acceptance trials were completed in 1975, about a year later than the Mi-24D's; both models were formally included into the inventory by the same Council of Ministers directive on 29th March 1976. The Mi-24V entered production in 1976 and was built in both Arsen'yev and Rostov. An export version with downgraded avionics was designated **Mi-35**. The reporting name for both was *Hind-E*. A dual-control **trainer version of the Mi-35** similar to the Mi-24DU (no separate designation is known) was supplied to the Indian Air Force; interestingly, there never was a 'Mi-24VU' for the Soviet Army. Overall, the two plants manufactured close to 1,500 Mi-24Vs/Mi-35s.

Improvements made in the course of Mi-24V production as a result of combat experience in Afghanistan included vortex-type intake filters to prevent excessive engine wear and foreign object damage (FOD) in dusty environments and an SPO-15LM *Beryoza* (Birch) radar homing and warning system (RHAWS) giving 360° coverage. Infra-red countermeasures (IRCM) equipment for protection against heat-seek-

'07 Orange', a Mi-24D serving with the 16th Air Army deployed in East Germany in the 1980s, parked on a perforated steel planking (PSP) hardstand. Note the unusual yellow colour of the normally red 'Excellent aircraft' maintenance award badge.

An early Mi-24V minus air intake filters. The mounting frames for 9M114 Shtoorm ATGM launch tubes and the Lipa IR jammer aft of the main rotor head are clearly visible.

ing missiles included four or six 32-round ASO-2V-02 flare launchers, an SOEP-V1A Lipa (Linden; pronounced ***lee**pah*; NATO *Hot Brick*) active IR jammer aft of the main rotor head and optional air/exhaust mixers to reduce the helicopter's heat signature. To improve survivability the fuel tanks were filled with explosion-suppression polyurethane foam, additional armour was fitted, extra valves were introduced to prevent total loss of hydraulic fluid in the event of damage and the tail rotor control rods were spaced wider apart to stop them from being severed by a single hit.

In 1975 the Mil' OKB brought out a derivative of the Mi-24V designated **Mi-24P** (***push**echnyy* – cannon-armed), or *izdeliye* 243. The machine-gun barbette gave place to a 30-mm (1.18 in) Gryazev/Shipunov GSh-30K twin-barrel rapid-firing cannon borrowed from the Sukhoi Su-25 *Frogfoot* attack aircraft. The weight and strong recoil of the cannon rendered it unsuitable for flexible installation, therefore it was installed rigidly on the starboard side of the forward fuselage; the pilot had to aim the cannon by turning the whole helicopter. Additionally, new 20-tube B-8V20A pods with 80-mm (3.14-in) S-8 unguided rockets were introduced. Development of the Mi-24P suffered delays owing to problems with the cannon installation: the powerful recoil of the cannon literally shook the avionics to pieces. Once the problem had been resolved, the Mi-24P entered production at both plants in 1981; more than 635 had been built when production ended in 1989. The export version was designated **Mi-35P**; the reporting name was *Hind-F*. In 2011 production of the Mi-35P at Rostvertol was reinstated.

A Mi-24V with intake filters and exhaust/air mixers seen during the Afghan War, with two 9M114 missiles fitted. Note that the tactical code '34' is only carried on a card in a cabin window.

A Mi-24P with four B-8V20 FFAR pods attached. The cannon barrels are visible on the starboard side of the nose. Note the distinctive 'cloverleaf' camouflage pattern and the unusual forward position of the tactical code '48 Red'.

Close-up of the Mi-24P's fixed twin-barrel GSh-2-30 cannon. Note also the RHAWS antenna fairings ahead of the cabin doors.

Russian Air Force Mi-24P '37 White' at Syzran' with four 450-litre drop tanks attached. Note the absence of intake filters, the simplified 'striped' camouflage and the new tri-colour star insignia.

A Russian Air Force Mi-24P based at Pugachov, with eagle nose art, 'Pugachov – Russia – 1st Helo Sqn' titles and Russian flag (but Soviet-style stars). Note the bird-scaring 'eyes' painted on the intake filters.

A pair of Mi-24Ps show off the triple ASO-2V flare dispensers on the fuselage sides. Note the unpainted APU cowling on '18 Yellow'.

The Mi-24P proved the expediency of fitting a cannon, but its combat efficiency was limited because the cannon was fixed. On the other hand, the GSh-30K was excessive for certain missions where a 23-mm cannon would do. Therefore a version designated **Mi-24VP** (*izdeliye* 258) was submitted for State acceptance trials in 1985. It differed from the Mi-24V in having a 23-mm Gryazev/Shipunov GSh-23L twin-barrel cannon in an NPPU-24 nose barbette; thus, the helicopter finally received the weapons fit envisaged by Mikhail L. Mil'. Mi-24VP production was limited to 25 examples built in 1989.

Special mission versions of the Mi-24 also emerged over the years. The **Mi-24R** (*raz**ved**chik* – reconnaissance [aircraft]), or *izdeliye* 2462, nuclear/biological/chemical (NBC) reconnaissance version appeared in late 1978; it could take air and soil samples and transmit the results to command posts via data link. The crew comprised a pilot, a navigator and two mission equipment operators. 110 production examples were built in 1983-89, whereupon the upgraded **Mi-24RA** was brought out with better mission and communications equipment and a reduced crew complement, leaving only one NBC reconnaissance operator. The reporting name was *Hind-G1*. The Mi-24R found use during damage control operations after the Chernobyl' nuclear disaster.

In 1979 the **Mi-24K** (*korrekti**rov**schchik*), or *izdeliye* 201, was developed for battlefield surveillance, tactical reconnaissance and artillery spotting. It featured an Iris wide-angle optical sensor system under the nose and a Ruta reconnaissance suite (comprising an optical target identification system, a computer and an intelligence processor) in the cabin, plus an AFA-100 oblique camera with a camera port on the starboard side. The mission equipment was controlled from the front cockpit. 92 such machines codenamed *Hind-G2* were built in 1983-89.

There were also various one-off versions. In 1973 the Mil' OKB brought out the **Mi-24BMT** (*booksi**rov**schchik* ***min**novo* ***trah**la*), or *izdelye* 248, mine countermeasures version equipped for towing a mine-clearing sled; however, the Mi-8BT proved more effective in the MCM role. In 1981 the OKB's Rostov branch created the **Mi-24TECh-24** version – a mobile repair shop for servicing/repairing other Mi-24s in the field. In the late 1980s a demilitarised Mi-24V was converted into an ecological survey aircraft for detecting oil spills, monitoring air pollution and the like. The sensors were mounted in the nose and in underwing pods; the equipment operator had the cabin all to himself. The aircraft was unveiled at the industry fair in Nizhniy Novgorod in 1991. In 1995 the **Mi-24PS** special operations helicopter (*pa**trool'**no-spa**sah**tel'nyy* – patrol/rescue, used attributively) was developed for the Russian police.

The Mi-24 was also used extensively for test and development work. Thus, in 1975 one of the V-24 prototypes was fitted with an experimental fenestron-type tail rotor, which turned out to be unsuitable for helicopters in this weight class. One of them, possibly an early-production Mi-24A was used to test a new main rotor developed for the Mi-28 *Havoc* attack helicopter, while another

A Mi-24VP with an NPPU-24 nose barbette mounting a GSh-23L twin-barrel cannon.

A Russian Navy/Baltic Fleet Mi-24VP armed with a pair of GUV pods configured with triple Gatling machine-guns.

A Mi-24R NBC reconnaissance helicopter shows off its distinguishing features – the 'clutching hand' soil samplers at the wingtips, the ventral air sampling intake and the bulged observation windows.

'14 Yellow', an operational Mi-24R assigned to a 16th Air Army unit in East Germany.

served as a testbed for the Mi-28's squashed-X tail rotor. Two Mi-24Vs became testbeds for the *Havoc*'s PrPNK-28 navigation/attack suite. In May 2000 a Mi-24 was converted into a testbed for the Klimov VK-2500 turboshaft – the latest version of the proven TV3-117.

In 1975 a pre-production V-24 was stripped of all unnecessary items (including the stub wings) for an attempt on the Class E world speed and time-to-height records; in the documents submitted to the International Aeronautical Federation (FAI) the helicopter was called A-10. On 16th July a female crew captained by Galina Rastorgooyeva reached 341.35 km/h (211.98 mph) on a 15/25-km (9.31/15.52-mile) closed circuit, attaining 334.464 km/h (207.74 mph) over a 100-km (62.11-mile) course two days later. On 1st August 1975 Lyudmila Polyanskaya set another female record – 331.023 km/h (205.59 mph) over a 500-km (310.55-mile) course. A week later Rastorgooyeva reached 3,000 m (9,843 ft) in 2 minutes 33.5 seconds in the A-10; on 13th August she attained 333 km/h (206.83 mph) over a 1,000-km (621.12-mile) course. Another time-to-height record was achieved on 26th August – 6,000 m (19,685 ft) in 7 minutes 43 seconds. On 21st September 1978 Gurghen

The Russian Air Force's upgraded Mi-24PN features clipped wings with new pylons, a fixed landing gear and a Zarevo thermal imager/laser ranger on a distinctive 'proboscis' in the nose.

A flight of four Mi-24PNs makes a demo flight at the Flying Legends event at Monino, Russia, in 2005.

R. Karapetian set an absolute world speed record for helicopters (368.4 km/h; 229 mph), which stood until 1986.

Development of the *Hind* did not stop with the end of production. The Mil' Company and Rostvertol strove to improve the chopper, developing various upgrades and service life extension programmes for the existing fleet of Mi-24s both in Russia and abroad. Another factor was that Russia's economic troubles of the 1990s and the resulting defence budget cuts had caused new hardware deliveries to the Russian Armed Forces to dry up, and the existing fleet had to be maintained. The upgrades focus on giving the helicopter round-the-clock capability, improving flight performance and integrating new weapons. The first programme for the *Hind-E/F* launched in the mid-1990s was the **Mi-24VM** and **Mi-24PM** (offered for export as the **Mi-35M** and **Mi-35PM** respectively). This was a five-stage programme that could be implemented fully or in part to match the customer's requirements and wallet. In 'full option' configuration the Mi-24VM/Mi-35M had the rotor system of the Mi-28, featuring a hingeless main rotor hub with elastomeric bearings, glassfibre blades and a squashed-X four-blade tail rotor. The helicopter was powered by Klimov VK-2500 engines optimised for high altitudes, with a 2,700-shp contingency rating which ensured continued flight in the event of an engine failure. To save weight the undercarriage was fixed and the stub wings were clipped outboard of the outer pylons; the pylons were new, with multiple weapons racks permitting carriage of four-packs of ATGMs. In similar manner to the Mi-24VP, an NPPU-24 or NPPU-23 cannon barbette was fitted, mounting an air-cooled GSh-23L or a water-cooled GSh-23V respectively, with 450 rounds. New weapons were integrated: in lieu of 9M114 Shtoorm ATGMs the Mi-24VM could carry up to 16 9M120 *Ataka* (Attack) ATGMs, as well as up to four 9M39 *Igla-V* (Needle-V) IR-homing AAMs. The unguided weapons range was complemented by two B-13L1 pods, each holding five 122-mm (4.8-in) S-13 unguided rockets. The existing analogue computers were replaced by a BVK-24 digital data processing suite; also, the cockpits featured liquid-crystal multi-function displays, night vision goggles (NVG) were integrated, and a Urals gyrostabilised optoelectronic 'turret' with thermal imaging, LLLTV and laser ranger channels was installed on the starboard side of the nose.

The Mi-35M had its début at the 41st Paris Aerospace Salon in 1995; however, it was not until 4th March 1999 that the Mi-24VM entered flight test. Since then the upgraded helicopter has been displayed at various airshows in various configurations with Russian or western avionics and weapons. Several orders were secured; e.g., the Cyprus National Guard Air Wing had its *Hind-Fs* converted to Mi-35PMs. In 2011 the Rostvertol plant began manufacturing new-build Mi-35Ms – both for the Russian Air Force and for export. The Russian examples have indigenous ONV-2 NVG and a Urals Optomechanical Plant (UOMZ) GOES-342 optoelectronic 'turret'.

Before that, however, a cheaper upgrade designated **Mi-24PN** was developed by Rostvertol. It had the fixed gear, clipped wings

A nice shot of a cruising Mi-24PN. Interestingly, *Hinds* upgraded to this standard lack intake filters.

and ability to carry Ataka ATGMs but featured a ***Zarevo*** (Glow) gyrostabilised thermal imaging system developed by the Krasnogorsk Mechanical Plant, plus Gheofizika ONV-1 NVG. Development was completed in October 2000, whereupon Rostvertol upgraded a number of Mi-24Ps for the Russian Army Aviation. Unfortunately, the Zarevo system had no growth potential. Therefore in 2000 the Mil' Company started work on the **Mi-24VK-1** and **Mi-24VK-2** night-capable versions of the *Hind-E*; the former utilised some French electronic components while the other one had fully indigenous avionics (the appropriately modified *Hind-F* was designated **Mi-24PK-2**). The Aviakon helicopter repair plant in the Ukraine has developed its own *Hind-F* upgrade for the Ukrainian Armed Forces – the **Mi-24PU1** which has TV3-117VMA-SBM1V-02 engines with a 2,000-shp maximum continuous rating, an Adros KT-01AV IR jammer, an FPM-01KV laser target designator and western GPS and communications equipment. Various upgrades of the Mi-24 have also been performed outside the CIS (in Poland, Israel, the UK etc.); the most radical is the **SuperHind Mk III/Mk IV** offered by the South African company Advanced Technologies and Engineering (ATE) in 1998.

This upgraded *Hind* may be a prototype of the Mi-35M, featuring clipped wings and a GSh-23L movable cannon but retaining the retractable landing gear and the old Raduga-Sh targeting system. Eight-packs of 9M120 Ataka ATGMs are suspended on the outer pylons, while the inner ones carry paired 9M39 Igla-V AAMs.

Above: '56 Yellow', a new-build Mi-35M for the Russian Air Force, shows off the new main and tail rotors identical to those of the Mi-28, the new-style slate grey colour scheme, the clipped wings and fixed gear.

Below: '54 Yellow', a new-build Mi-35M for the Russian Air Force. The optoelectronic 'ball turret' on the starboard side of the nose is well visible. The digits of the RF- registration have yet to be added.

THE Mi-24 IN ACTION

Mi-24A deliveries to the Soviet Air Force commenced in 1970. The helicopter regiment in Chernigovka (Far Eastern Military District) was the first service unit to master the *Hind*. It was soon followed by units based at Brody (Carpathian MD), Pruzhany (Belorussian MD), Mogocha (Transbaikalian MD), Raukhovka (Odessa MD) and the like. In addition to home ground, Soviet Mi-24s were stationed in Eastern Europe. The Mi-24 served with the Group of Soviet Forces in Germany from 1972 until the Russian pullout in 1994. Soviet Mi-24 units in Germany reported to two tank armies and three mechanised armies, operating from Allstedt, Brandis, Dresden-Hellerau, Hassleben, Jüterbog-Altes Lager, Mahlwinkel, Neuruppin, Parchim, Sperenberg, Stendal, Templin, Weimar-Nohra and Werneuchen. Soviet Army *Hinds* also served with the Northern Group of Forces in Poland; the only known base is Bagicz.

In the mid-1970s the rotary-wing element of the Air Force was reorganised as the Army Aviation. By the early 1980s it had about 15 independent combat helicopter regiments reporting to the HQs of mechanised or tank armies, each unit having two *Hind* squadrons and a single Mi-8TV squadron. Additionally, Mi-24s were operated by independent combat control squadrons assigned to mechanised or armoured divisions. The *Hind*'s 'responsibilities' were close air support (CAS) for ground forces and assault groups airlifted by transport helicopters, tank-busting and destruction of enemy strongholds, insertion and extraction of commando groups, casualty evacuation, and destruction of low- and slow-flying aerial targets, notably other helicopters.

The pilots were generally pleased with the Mi-24's handling and agility, which was surprising for a helicopter of this size and weight. Yet the *Hind* had its share of teething troubles; it was not before the Mi-24V entered service that the Army Aviation got a dependable tank-buster. Because of the extensive glazing the Mi-24A was promptly dubbed *veranda* or *sta**kan*** (drinking glass); however, the lean predatory silhouette and camouflage soon gave rise to a new nickname, *kroko**dil*** (crocodile), which accompanies the *Hind* to this day.

Before the Soviet Union's collapse the Mi-24/-25/-35 was exported to more than 20 countries, including some Warsaw Pact nations (Czechoslovakia, East Germany, Hungary and Poland), Afghanistan, Algeria, Angola, Ethiopia, India, Iraq, Libya, Mozambique, Nicaragua, North Korea, North and South Yemen, Peru, Syria, Vietnam and the like. More recent customers include Indonesia, Venezuela, Brazil and Cyprus.

The Mi-24 has taken part in than more than 30 conflicts of varying scale, so one may safely call it the world's most battle-proven combat helicopter. It drew first blood in 1978 when Ethiopian *Hinds* took part in repelling the Somalian aggression. The most famous conflict in which the Mi-24 participated was undoubtedly the Afghan War of 1980-89. The *Hinds* were involved in the war from Day One; they flew 'lower, slower and over shorter distances than anyone else', but were often more effective in the strike role than jet fighter-bombers. The main elements of *Hind* tactics were typical of Soviet military philosophy: surprise action, uninterrupted engagement of the enemy

A pair of Mi-24Vs attacks a target with S-8 unguided rockets fired from B-8V20 pods.

A Mi-24V equipped with exhaust/air mixers and armed with UB-32A FFAR pods awaits the next mission at a base in Afghanistan. The *Hind* formed the backbone of the 40th Army's rotary-wing force during the Afghan War.

and mutual protection of the attacking forces.

In June 1980 eight Mi-24Ds toting big bombs played a vital role in the capture of Mt. Sanghi-Douzdan (the 'Mountain of Thieves') near Faïzabad which was a major Mujahideen guerrilla base. August 1980 was the first time when Mi-24s used fuel/air explosives against the Mujahideen. These munitions were none too reliable, but when they did work properly they were a terrifying weapon – it was not for nothing they have been called 'the poor man's nuke'. *Hinds* were often used to patrol areas of interest and destroy targets of opportunity, such as enemy supply convoys; such armed reconnaissance missions were usually flown in pairs or flights. From the summer of 1980 the *Hinds* were tasked with another important mission – escorting vehicle convoys bringing fuel, ammunition, food and the like for the Soviet contingent.

The *Hind*'s protection against AA fire was generally considered to be adequate. For a long time its most potent adversaries in Afghanistan were heavy machine-guns and AA guns which accounted for 42% and 25% of all Mi-24 losses respectively. When the enemy started using man-portable air defence systems (MANPADS) – Blowpipe, Redeye and Stinger missiles, losses mounted. This led the Mil' OKB to introduce air/exhaust mixers (which became obligatory on the Afghan TO in 1983), four chaff/flare dispensers (six from 1987 onwards) and the active IR jammer. An important mission of the Mi-24s was to provide protection for Soviet Air Force transports airlifting personnel, especially during the Soviet pullout. Each transport was escorted by a two pairs of *Hinds* on the lookout for Mujahideen positions. Sometimes a third pair followed close behind, firing IRCM flares to divert a possible Stinger attack until the airlifter was safe.

The Iran-Iraq War of 1980-1988 became another major chapter in the *Hind*'s career. Iraqi Mi-24As and Mi-25s were used for a variety of tasks, including destruction of soft-skinned and armoured vehicles, emplacements and bridges, escorting heliborne assaults, CAS, mine laying, reconnaissance/artillery spotting and even chemical warfare. In the course of the war there were 118 aircraft/helicopter engagements and 56 helicopter/helicopter engagements, including ten between Iraqi *Hinds* and Iranian Bell AH-1J Sea Cobras. The world's first helicopter duel took place in November 1980 when two Sea Cobras attacked a pair of Mi-24s with TOW ATGMs, destroying both *Hinds*. The Iraqi Mi-24 scored their first 'kill' of an AH-1 on 14th September 1983. The last engagement between the two types was on 22nd May 1986 when a Sea Cobra was destroyed; the overall 'kill' ratio was 10:6 in favour of the *Hind*. However, the most remarkable 'kill' of the war took place on 27th October 1982 when an Iraqi Mi-25 shot down an Iranian McDonnell Douglas F-4D Phantom II fighter.

Libyan Mi-25s saw action in the civil war in Chad (1980-87), supporting Goukouni Oueddei's pro-Libyan rebels opposing the regime of Hissène Habré; more recently they have been used by both sides in the Libyan civil war of 2011 which ended in the fall of Muammar Qaddafi's regime. Syrian Mi-25s were actively used against Israeli tanks during the 1982 war in Lebanon. In Angola, *Hinds* have been used against the UNITA rebels in three civil wars (1975-91, 1992-94 and 1998-2002). Other notable conflicts in which the type was involved are the Sri Lankan civil war (from 1995 to 2009), the 'Contra War' in Nicaragua (1981-89), the war in the former Yugoslavia and other hot spots of the world.

Sadly enough, the Mi-24 has also seen a lot of action in on the home front. Shortly before the breakup of the Soviet Union a spate of ethnic conflicts erupted; the first of these was in the Nagornyy Karabakh

Two Soviet Mi-24Ps carrying a pair of B-8V20 pods and a pair of 9M114 ATGMs each taxi out at an Afghan airbase with a taxiway surfaced with PSP.

enclave, the subject of a long-standing territorial dispute between Armenia and Azerbaijan. At first, Soviet Army Mi-24s patrolled the frontlines, escorting vehicle convoys and transport helicopters and suppressing *illegal armed units*. When the Soviet Union disintegrated and the Armenian leaders of Nagornyy Karabakh proclaimed sovereignty (recognised only by Armenia) on 2nd September 1991, both the Armenians and the Azeris took possession of about a dozen *Hinds* and used them against each other. The Mi-24 was used in the civil wars in Georgia (1991-92 and 1992-93) and Tajikistan (1992). However, the most notorious case is the two Chechen Wars (1994-96 and 1999-2001). While helicopter operations in the first war were rather limited, in the second campaign Army Aviation assets were used much more extensively, despite the foul weather common in those parts, and combat efficiency was also higher – although it was hampered by the *Hinds'* obsolescent avionics and lack of night capability. The Mi-24s were used to destroy guerrilla strongholds (especially in mountainous areas), escort Mi-8s inserting tactical assault groups and performing resupply operations and fly 'free chase' sorties, searching for targets of opportunity (suspicious vehicle convoys, illegal mini-refineries etc.). Unfortunately, losses could not be avoided, given that the guerrillas were not short of anti-aircraft weapons. In the Second Chechen War, between April 1999 and June 2000 alone Russian Army Aviation lost eleven Mi-24s. Even now, it has not proved possible to eradicate the bandits who, supported by the al-Qaeda terrorist network, have now moved into the neighbouring republic of Daghestan.

At present the *Hind* continues to form the backbone of Army Aviation of Russia, other CIS states and a number of other countries. To this day the Mi-24/-35 ranks among the most effective weapon systems in the arsenals of many nations. The helicopters (including the latest Mi-35Ms) are being actively used in anti-terrorist operations in the North Caucasus and Central Asia.

Soviet servicemen in field uniform and load-bearing jackets pose with a Mi-24 in Afghanistan.

A Soviet Mi-24P ('07 Red') with exhaust/air mixers flies over the snow-capped mountains of Afghanistan.

A Mi-24V flies over the outskirts of Kabul on a routine mission.

A 205th Independent Helicopter Sqn Mi-24V shot down over Afghanistan on 16th February 1988.

A gunner manning a PKT 7.62-mm machine-gun near a Mi-24's cabin window in Afghanistan.

Armourers hook up a 9M114 Shtoorm-V missile in its disposable launch tube to a 50th OSAP Mi-24 in 1986. Such missiles were occasionally used against Mujahideen air defence assets.

A ground crewman arms the ASO-2V flare dispensers of a Mi-24D which has been retrofitted with exhaust/air mixers and Lipa IR jammer for operations on the Afghan TO.

A Russian Air Force Mi-24V operating with Russian peacekeepers in Georgia in the 2000s, hence the blue stripe with MS (*mirotvorcheskiye seely* – peacekeeping force) titles.

THE Mi-24 IN DETAIL

The following brief description applies to the Mi-24V.

The fuselage is an all-metal semi-monocoque structure built in four sections. The *forward fuselage* (frames 1N-6N) is the crew section featuring armour plating integrated into the load-bearing structure. It includes tandem cockpits for the WSO and the pilot, with a walkway from the rear cockpit to the cabin. The cockpits are enclosed by teardrop canopies with bulletproof windshields and accessed via an upward-hinged section to port (front cockpit) and a car-type door to starboard (rear cockpit). The pilot's seat back and headrest are armoured; the seat pans are dished to take a parachute. Frame 1N carries the machine-gun barbette, with an ammunition box to starboard (frames 1N-4N); avionics and air conditioning system bays are located to port (frames 3N-4N). The nosewheel well is between frames 4N and 1. The *centre fuselage* (frames 1-15) incorporates the troop cabin (frames 1-8) accessed via horizontally-split doors on both sides, with the engines and main gearbox above it. The cabin has four windows on each side. Aft of the cabin the fuselage incorporates wing attachment fittings, an equipment bay, fuel tankage and the mainwheel wells (frames 8-12). The detachable *tailboom* of quasi-elliptical cross-section has 11 frames and terminates in the *tail rotor pylon* swept back 42°30' at quarter-chord. Variable-incidence stabilisers with a symmetrical airfoil are installed at the base of the fin. They are single-spar structures with six ribs; the skin is metal ahead of the spar and fabric elsewhere.

The tapered cantilever shoulder-mounted wings have 8°50' leading-edge sweep, 12° anhedral and 19° incidence. They are all-metal, two-spar stressed-skin structures with nine ribs each. Each wing is attached to the fuselage by four bolts and features two pylons; the downturned vertical endplates serve as attachment points for ATGM racks.

The hydraulically-retractable tricycle landing gear comprises a castoring levered-suspension nose unit with twin 400x200 mm (15.74x7.87 in) non-braking wheels and main units with single 720x320 mm (28.3x12.6 in) wheels and pneumatic rakes. Wheel track 3.03 m (9 ft 11 19/64 in), wheelbase 4.39 m (14 ft 4 53/64 in). Steering on the ground is by differential braking. All units retract aft (the mainwheels stow vertically almost at 90° to the direction of flight) and have oleo-pneumatic shock absorbers. The mainwheel wells are closed by twin doors, the rear ones opening only when the gear is in transit; the nosewheel well is closed by a single door, the wheels remaining semi-exposed when retracted. A non-retractable tail bumper is provided.

The Mi-24V is powered by two Izotov TV3-117V turboshafts with a nominal rating of 1,700 shp and a 2,200-shp take-off/contingency rating. The TV3-117V is a single-spool turboshaft with a 12-stage axial compressor, an annular combustion chamber, a two-stage axial turbine, a two-stage free turbine and an angled jetpipe through which the power output shaft passes. Starting is by means of an air starter using compressed air from an Ivchenko AI-9V auxiliary power unit installed aft of the main gearbox. The port and starboard engines are interchangeable, except for the jetpipes; Mi-24Vs built from 1984 onwards (with provisions for air/exhaust mixers) have identical jetpipes that are turned 180° for port/starboard side installation. The engine and main gearbox cowlings double as work platforms for maintenance and incorporate 8-mm (0⁵⁄₁₆ in) steel armour. Two fire extinguisher bottles are installed in the main gearbox bay, with flame sensors in the engine bays, the APU bay and the Nos. 1, 2 and 3 fuel tank containers.

Engine torque is fed into the VR-24 three-stage main gearbox which conveys torque to the main rotor, the accessories gearbox and the oil cooler fan. A drive shaft inside the tailboom connects the accessories gearbox to an intermediate gearbox at the base of the tail rotor pylon; thence a short shaft runs to the final drive gearbox. A rotor brake is provided.

The five-blade *main rotor* turns clockwise when seen from above. The fully articulated rotor head has flapping and drag hinges and is equipped with dampers. The constant-chord blades have an extruded aluminium alloy box spar of partial airfoil section to which 18 duralumin blade pockets with honeycomb filler are bonded. The three-blade tractor-type *tail rotor* installed on the port side also turns clockwise when seen from the hub. The constant-chord blades are of similar design but the blade pockets are made of glassfibre.

The Mi-24 has conventional mechanical flight controls, mostly with push-pull rods; cables are used for controlling the stabilisers, rotor brake and (partly) the tail rotor. Pitch and roll control, climb and descent are effected by the swashplate; directional control is effected by changing the tail rotor pitch. The swashplate is linked to the stabilisers whose incidence is adjusted automatically from 7°40' to –12°30'to match the flight speed, creating a longitudinal trim force. Four KAU-110 irreversible hydraulic actuators are included into the control circuits. An SAU-V24-1 automatic flight control system with a VUAP-1 autopilot provides autostabilisation in pitch, yaw, bank, speed and barometric altitude.

Fuel is carried in five self-sealing bag tanks below and aft of the cabin; total capacity is 2,130 litres (468.6 Imp. gal). An inert gas pressurisation system reduces the risk of fire and explosion in the event of battle damage; from the early 1980s onwards the tanks are filled with explosion-suppression polyurethane foam. Refuelling is by gravity via two filler caps. All four wing pylons are 'wet', permitting carriage of 450-litre (99 Imp. gal) drop tanks; a 1,250-litre (275 Imp. gal) ferry tank may be installed in the troop cabin.

There are three independent hydraulic systems. The main and backup systems work the control system actuators; the main system is also used for emergency landing gear extension. The auxiliary system operates the landing gear, tail rotor pitch governor, rudder pedal damper and the targeting system window's protective doors. The systems are operated by individual NP92A-4 variable delivery rate pumps driven off the accessories gearbox.

AC power (single-phase 36 V/50 Hz, single-phase 115 V/400 Hz, three-phase 36 V/400 Hz and three-phase 208 V/400 Hz) is supplied by two GT40PCh6 generators driven off the accessories gearbox. 27 DC power is provided by the APU's STG-3 starter-generator, with two 12SAM-28 (28 A·h) silver-zinc batteries as a backup. Emergency AC power supply is by PO-750A single-phase

The GSh-30K cannon of a Mi-24P with the cowling open.

The Zarevo thermal imager/laser ranger of a Mi-24PN.

converters (115 V) and PT-125Ts three-phase converters (36 V). The pneumatic system operates the wheel brakes, cockpit/cabin pressurisation seals and windshield washer. The rotor blade leading edges, windscreens and pitot heads are electrically de-iced; the engines have their own de-icing system, with hot-air de-icing for the inlets, hot oil de-icing for the front compressor bearing struts and electric de-icing for the intake filters.

The cockpits and troop cabin are air-conditioned and pressurised by engine bleed air. The air conditioning system ensures comfortable conditions at ambient temperatures of –50° to +37°C (–58° to +99°F). For operations above 3,000 m (9,840 ft) the Mi-24 has two 7.6-litre (1.672 Imp. gal) oxygen bottles. The crew uses KP-21 and KP-58 breathing apparatus with KM-16N oxygen masks; when the helicopter is used in the MEDEVAC role, two additional 7.6-litre oxygen bottles are provided.

Navigation equipment includes ARK-15M and ARK-U2 automatic direction finders, a Greben'-1 automatic approach system, an RV-5 radio altimeter and a DISS-15D Doppler speed/drift sensor. Communications equipment comprises an R-863 UHF command radio, a Yadro-M24 communications radio, an R-828 Evkalipt UHF radio for communicating with ground forces and an SPU-8 intercom. The crew is provided with R-855UM emergency radios facilitating SAR in the event of a crash.

An SRO-1P Parol' IFF transponder is provided. ESM and IRCM equipment comprises an SPO-15LM RHAWS, four ASO-2V chaff/flare dispensers under the tailboom (or six ASO-2Vs on the rear fuselage sides), and a SOEP-V1A active IR jammer.

The Mi-24V has a USPU-24 powered barbette with a 12.7-mm YakB-12,7 four-barrel Gatling machine-gun traversable through +20°/–40° in elevation and ±60° in azimuth. The weapon has a rate of fire of 4,000-4,500 rounds per minute, with an ammo capacity of 1,470 rounds. The barbette is slaved to a KPS-53AV sighting system; there is also an ASP-17V collimator gunsight for the pilot.

The Mi-24V uses 9M114 Shtoorm-V supersonic ATGM with SACLOS guidance. Normally, two or four are carried on the wing endplates (optionally, four more on the outer pylons). The 9M114 has a calibre of 130 mm (5.12 in), a 6-kg (13.22-lb) warhead capable of penetrating 560-mm (2.2 in) armour and weighs 31.8 kg (70.1 lb); kill range is 800-5,000 m (0.49-3.1 miles). A Raduga-Sh targeting/guidance system comprising LLLTV, FLIR and command link equipment caters for the missiles.

Unguided air-to-ground weapons (aimed by means of the KPS-53AV system) are up to four UB-32A-73 pods with thirty-two 57-mm (2.24-in) S-5KO, S-5KP or S-5MO FFARs each, or four free-fall bombs of 50-/100-/250-kg (110-/220-/551-lb) calibre, or two 500-kg (1,102-lb) bombs or ZB-500GD napalm tanks. The Mi-24 can use a mix of bombs and rockets; in this case the FFAR pods are carried on the inboard stations. Other external stores options are two KMGU-2 dispensers with anti-tank or anti-personnel mines, or two UPK-23-250 pods (containing a GSh-23 cannon with 250 rounds), or two GUV (9A669) pods, each with either two 7.62-mm (.30 calibre) GShG-7,62 four-barrel Gatling machine-guns plus one YakB-12,7 machine gun or one 30-mm (1.18 calibre) AGS-17 Plamya automatic grenade launcher. The pods are carried on the inboard stations only. Provisions are made for carrying R-60 (AA-8 *Aphid*) short-range IR-homing air-to-air missiles for self-defence.

Mi-24 FAMILY BASIC DATA

	Mi-24A	Mi-24D	Mi-24V	Mi-24P	Mi-24VM
Powerplant	2 x TV3-117 2 x 2,200 shp	2 x TV3-117 2 x 2,200 shp	2 x TV3-117V 2 x 2,225 shp	2 x TV3-117V 2 x 2,225 shp	2 x TV3-117VM 2 x 2,500 shp
Main rotor diameter	17.3 m (56 ft 9 7/64 in)	17.3 m (56 ft 9 7/64 in)	17.3 m (56 ft 9 7/64 in)	17.3 m (56 ft 9 7/64 in)	17.2 m (56 ft 5 7/64 in)
Tail rotor diameter	3.908 m (12 ft 9 55/64 in)	3.908 m (12 ft 9 55/64 in)	3.908 m (12 ft 9 55/64 in)	3.908 m (12 ft 9 55/64 in)	3.84 m (12 ft 7 3/16 in)
Length with rotors turning	21.35 m (70 ft 0 1/2 in)	21.35 m (70 ft 0 1/2 in)	21.35 m (70 ft 0 1/2 in)	21.35 m (70 ft 0 1/2 in)	21.27 m (69 ft 9 13/32 in)
Height on ground (with tail rotor)	5.47 m (17 ft 11 23/64 in)	5.47 m (17 ft 11 23/64 in)	5.47 m (17 ft 11 23/64 in)	5.47 m (17 ft 11 23/64 in)	5.47 m (17 ft 11 23/64 in)
Wing span	6.54 m (21 ft 5 31/64 in)	6.54 m (21 ft 5 31/64 in)	6.54 m (21 ft 5 31/64 in)	6.54 m (21 ft 5 31/64 in)	4.765 m (15 ft 7 39/64 in)
Wing area, m^2 (sq. ft)	6.25 (67.2)	6.25 (67.2)	6.25 (67.2)	6.25 (67.2)	n.a.
Operating empty weight, kg (lb)	7,792 (17,178)	8,450 (18,628)	8,620 (19,003)	8,570	8,090 (17,835)
Normal TOW, kg (lb)	10,500 (23,150)	11,200 (24,690)	11,200 (24,690)	11,300	10,800 (23,810)
MTOW, kg (lb)	11,500 (25,350)	11,500 (25,350)	11,500 (25,350)	11,500 (25,350)	11,500 (25,350)
Maximum payload, kg (lb)	2,500 (5,510)	2,500 (5,510)	2,500 (5,510)	2,500 (5,510)	2,500 (5,510)
Top speed, km/h (mph)	310-330 (192-205)	310-330 (192-205)	310-330 (192-205)	320 (199)	312 (194)
Cruising speed, km/h (mph)	240-280 (149-173)	260-275 (161-170)	260-275 (161-170)	270 (167)	260 (162)
Hovering ceiling out of ground effect, ISA m (ft)	1,600 (5,250)	1,300 (4,260)	2,200 (7,217)	2,000 (6,560)	3,100 (10,170)
Service ceiling, m (ft)	5,120 (16,790)	4,500 (14,760)	4,600 (15,090)	4,500 (14,760)	5,750 (18,865)
Operational range, km (miles)	485 (301)	595 (370)	595 (370)	450 (280)	435 (270)
Ferry range, km (miles)	1,210 (752)	1,125 (699)	1,000 (621)	1,000 (621)	1,085 (674)

Side view of a V-24 prototype.

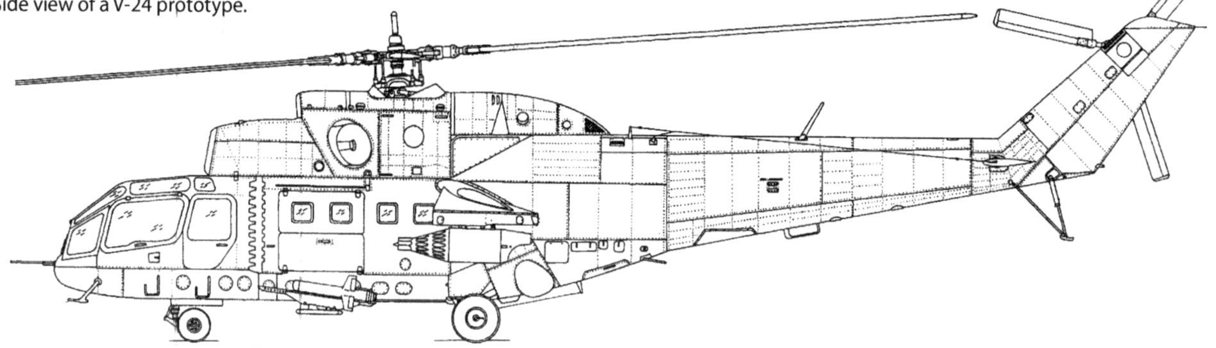

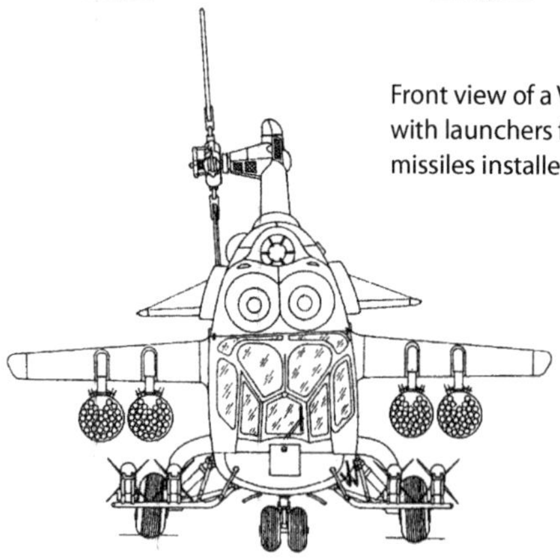

Front view of a V-24 prototype with launchers for 9M17M missiles installed.

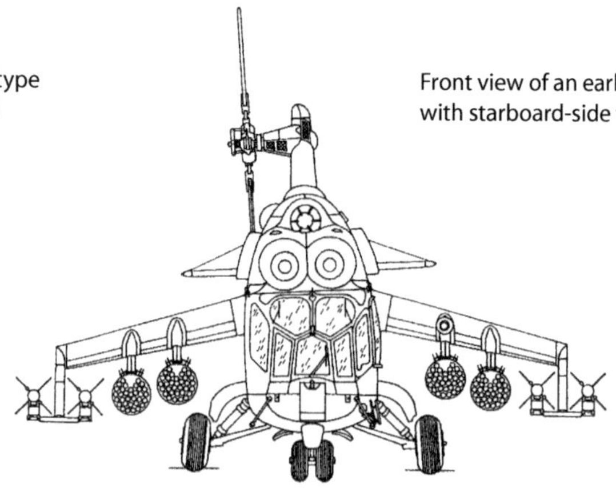

Front view of an early Mi-24A with starboard-side tail rotor.

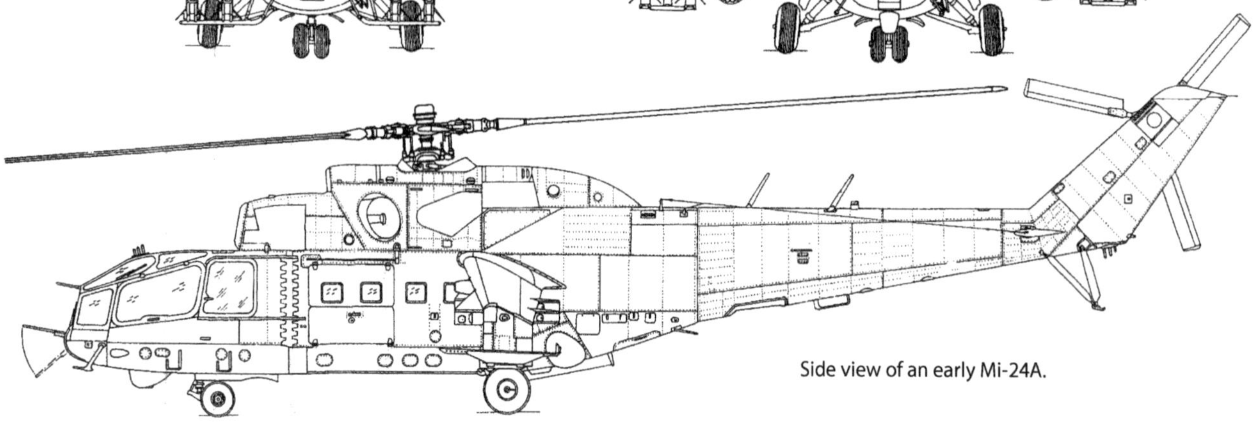

Side view of an early Mi-24A.

Side view of a Mi-24U trainer.

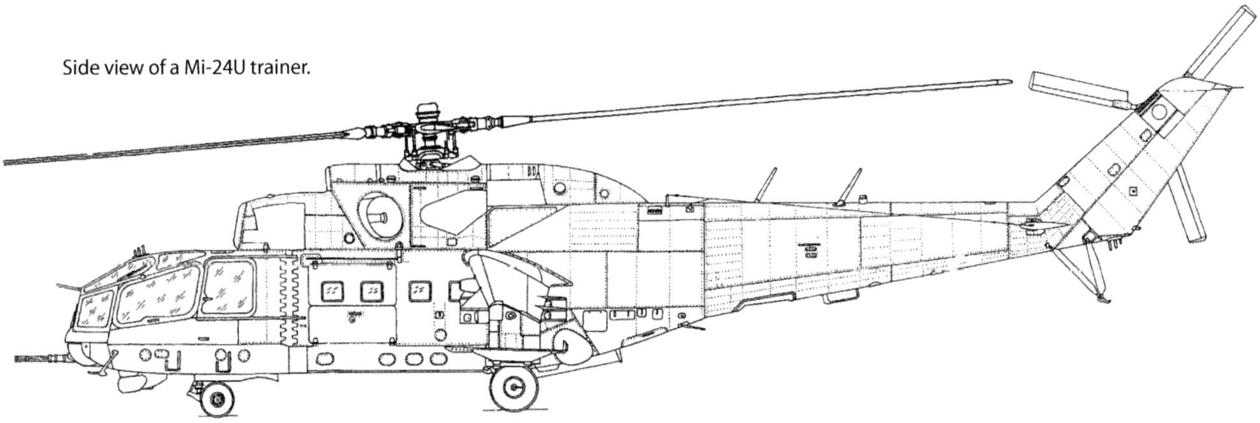

A Mi-24B development aircraft.

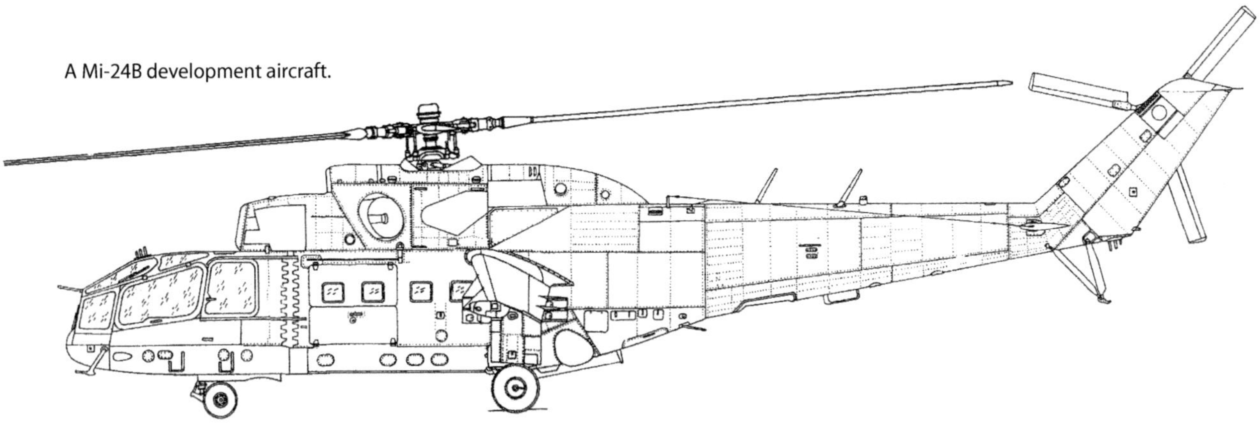

Side view of a Mi-24D armed with UB-32A FFAR pods.

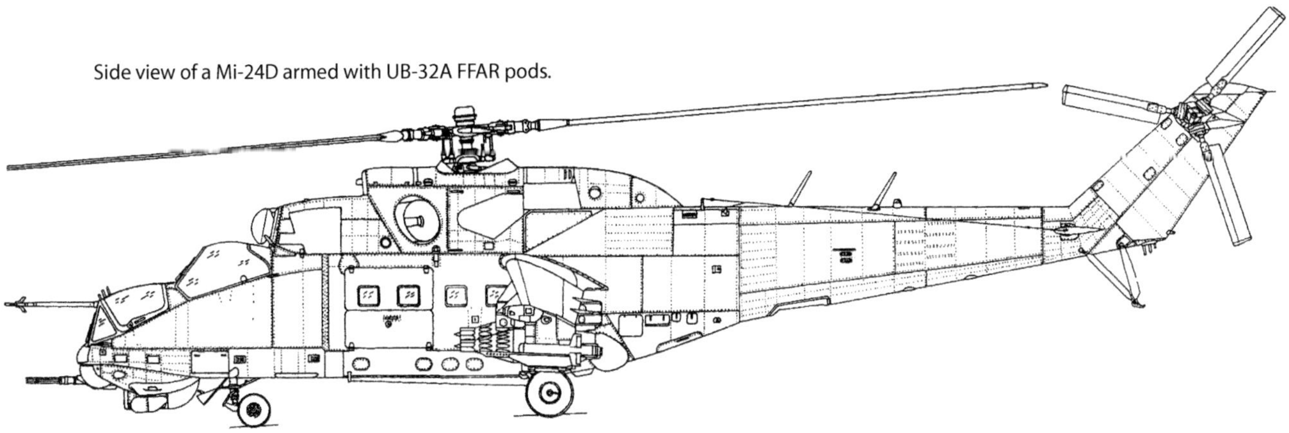

Side view of a Mi-24DU trainer.

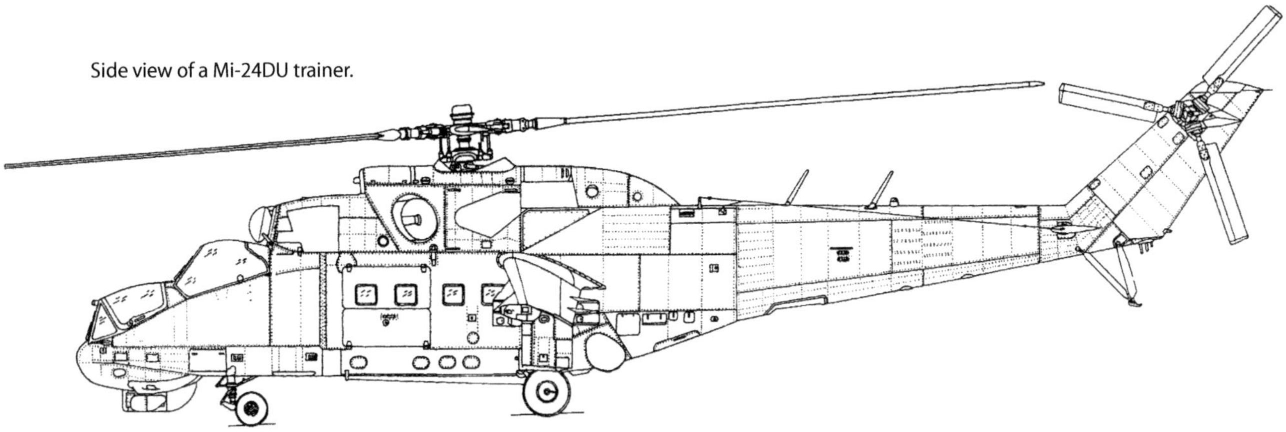

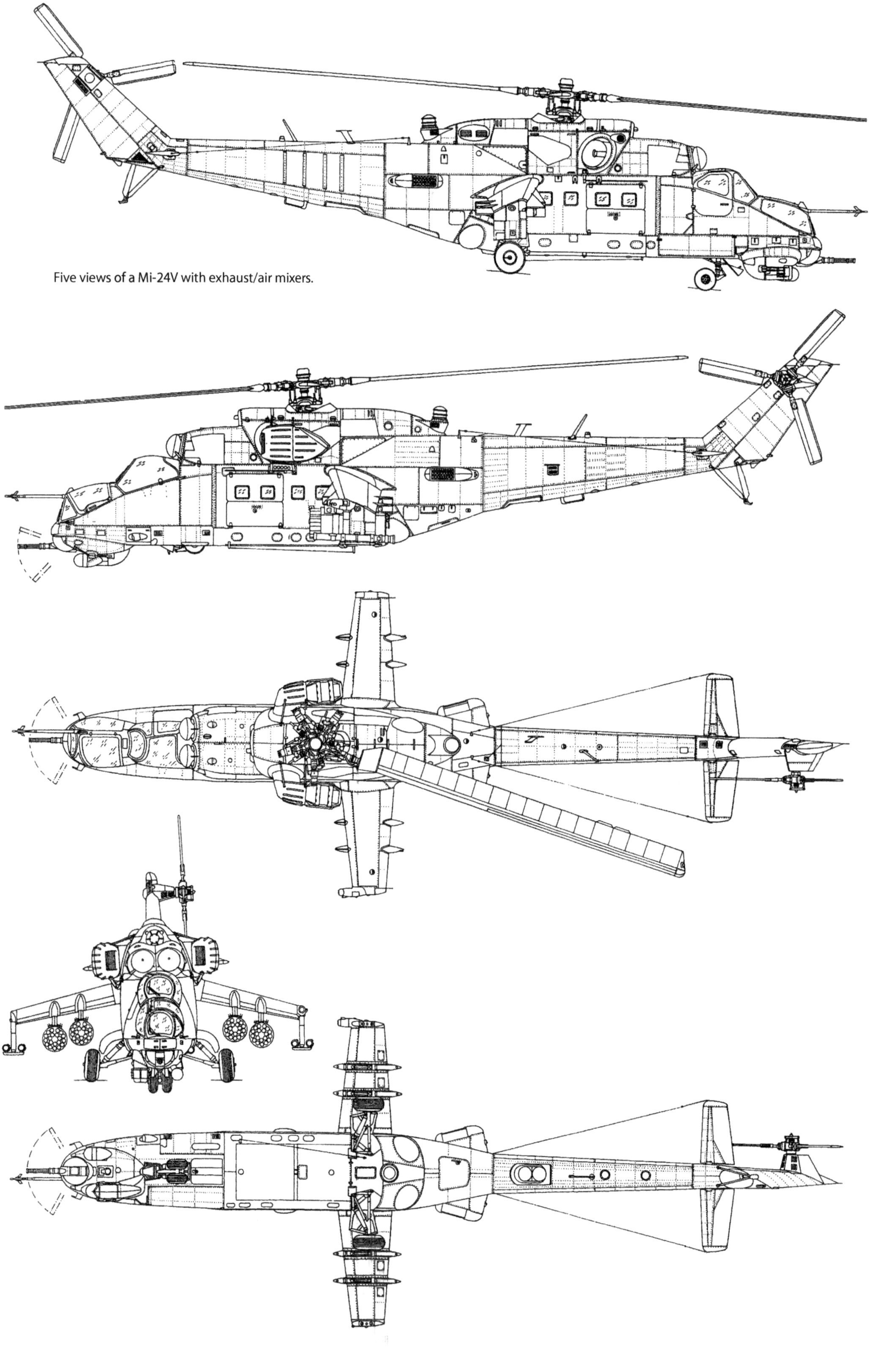

Five views of a Mi-24V with exhaust/air mixers.

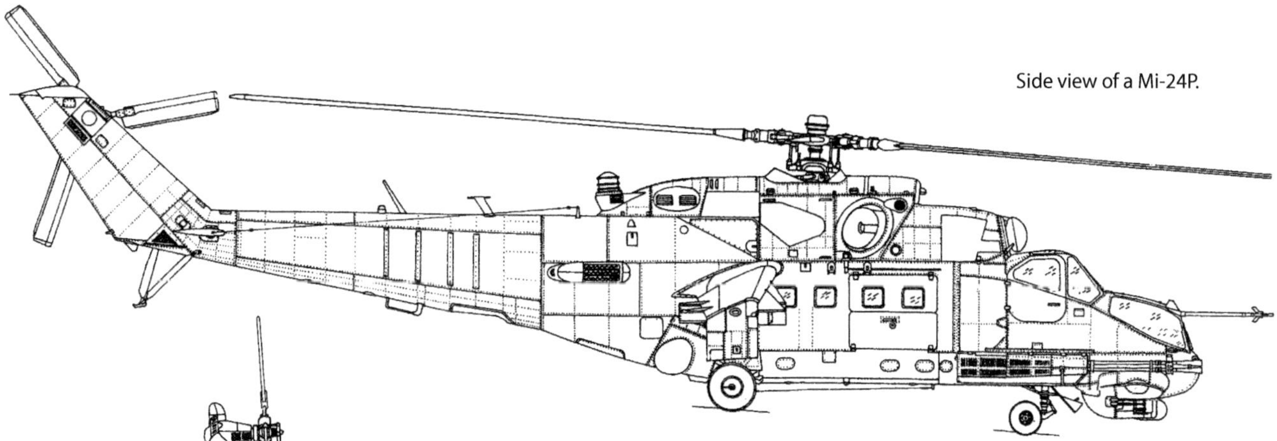

Side view of a Mi-24P.

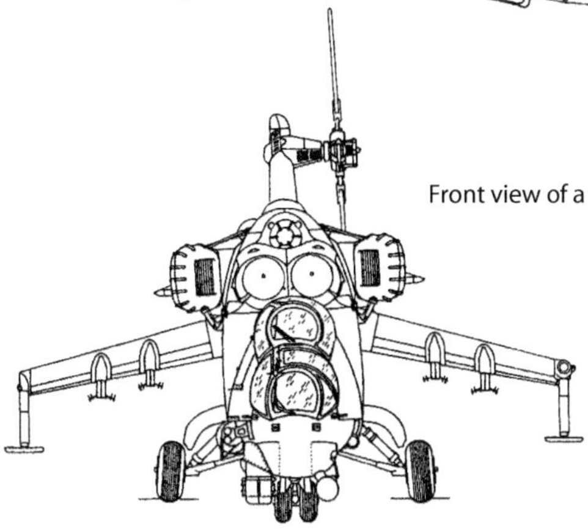

Front view of a Mi-24P.

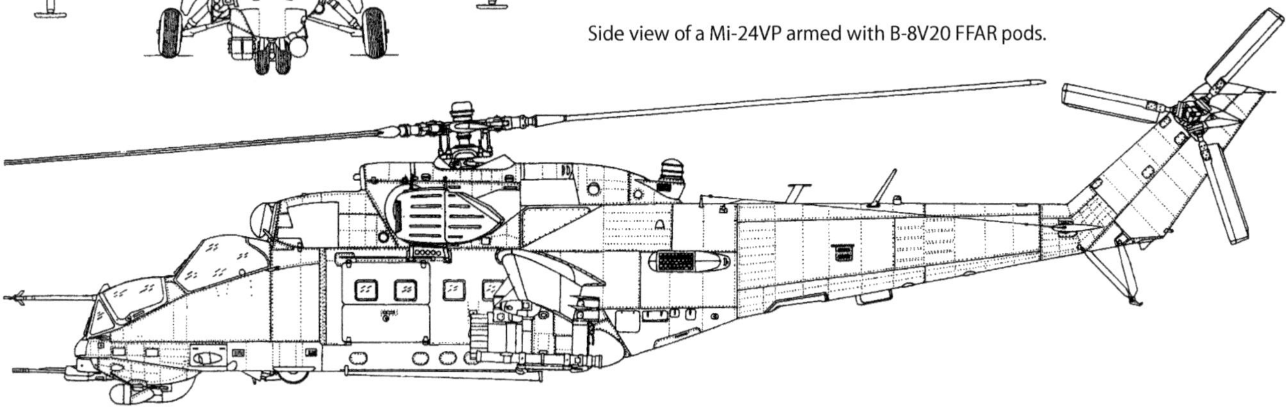

Side view of a Mi-24VP armed with B-8V20 FFAR pods.

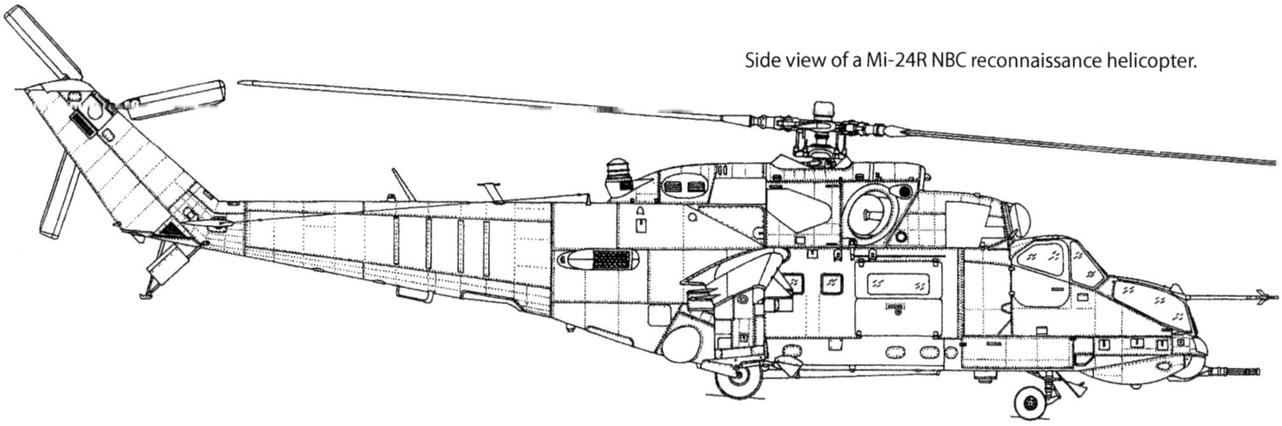

Side view of a Mi-24R NBC reconnaissance helicopter.

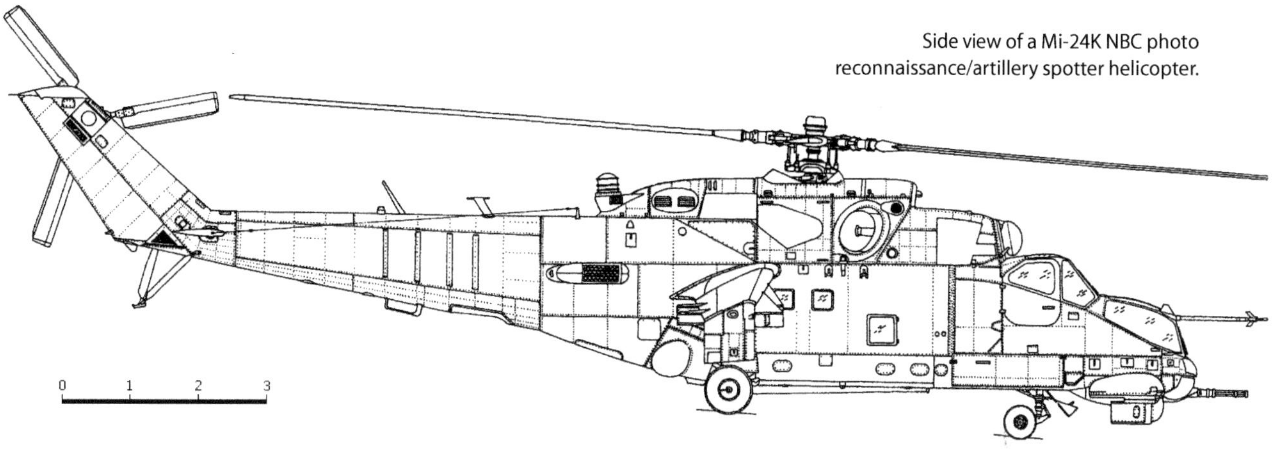

Side view of a Mi-24K NBC photo reconnaissance/artillery spotter helicopter.

The Modeller's Corner

MIL' **Mi-24** 1:72nd scale

The Mi-24 is a perennially popular subject with plastic kit manufacturers, and *Hinds* come in every shape and size – literally. In 1:72nd scale, the Mi-24 was first offered as an injection moulded kit in 1984 by **Airfix** (Mil Mi-24 Hind A/D, Ref. No. 05023); the kit was repackaged same year in the USA under the **MPC** brand (Ref. No. 1-4409). It allows you to build either the **Mi-24A** or the **Mi-24D**, with optional cockpit sections; the kit even lets you choose between the early or late *Hind-A* (with pusher or tractor tail rotor). The box contains three sprues with 132 parts and decals for a Soviet Air Force helicopter; the main components have raised panel lines. Accuracy is poor (the troop cabin is too far aft and has seats along the walls rather than on the centreline, the shape of the canopy and the main rotor blades is wrong etc.), and from today's standpoint the Airfix kit can only be described as trash. (Airfix also had a kit called '**Mi-24 Gunship**' which looked like a reissue of the above kit with decals for Soviet and Czechoslovak Air Force machines but had a separate reference number – (9)05017.) However, the kits are no longer available.

The French marque **Heller** also offered a 'two-in-one' **Mi-24A/Mi-24D** kit (Ref. No. 80369). The decal sheet lets you build a Soviet Mi-24A or an East German Mi-24D. There are unconfirmed reports that it is another iteration of the Airfix kit.

Hasegawa brought out a **Mi-24A** kit in its King series (Ref. No. 04019 or K-19) in 1986; it is no longer in production. This is a more accurate rendering of a late *Hind-A*, with more realistic proportions and finely engraved panel lines. The cabin doors on both sides can be opened; however, there are no troop seats which will have to be scratch-built. A major shortcoming of this and other Hasegawa *Hinds* is the incorrect main rotor blades which are too long and narrow; another gaffe is that the cockpit has three

The box top of Hasegawa's 1:72nd scale Mi-24A.

The Hasegawa Mi-24 built 'out of the box' by Austin Taylor. It was painted with Tamiya and Gunze Sangyo paints.

The box top of Airfix's 1:72nd scale Mi-24A.

An Airfix Mi-24A converted into a Mi-24B by a modeller with the internet alias Frog63. It is painted with Zvezda acrylic paints.

seats instead of two. The box contains 111 parts plus a few photo-etched (PE) parts. Again, the decals are for a Soviet example; the decal sheet includes correct 'Danger' stencils in Russian but incorrect instrument panels. There used to be one more **Mi-24A** kit on the Russian market under the **Alanger** brand (Ref. No. 072017), but this was a repackaging of the Heller kit.

A more recent offering is the **Mi-24A** by the Russian manufacturer **Zvezda** (Ref. No. 7273), and this is a new kit, *not* a repack. It is a fine kit with the portside canopy door, cabin doors and engine/main gearbox cowlings that can be opened, detailed engines and other niceties. The box contains 239 parts; the decal sheet features markings for a Soviet machine and an Afghan Air Force example with early red roundels.

Top: The box top of the new 1:72nd scale Mi-24A kit by Zvezda.

Above: Detail views of the assembled but unpainted model showing details of the engines, main gearbox and cockpit.

Right: The Zvezda Mi-24A built 'out of the box' by a modeller with the internet alias Redcat. The model was painted with Tamiya and Akan paints.

Above: Hasegawa's 1:72nd scale Mi-24D with the original box art.

Above: The box top of MPC's 1:72nd scale two-in-one *Hind* kit showing a Mi-24D.

Hasegawa also offered a **Mi-24D** kit (Ref. No. 04020 or K-20); unfortunately the fuselage is about 10 mm too short and lacks the distinctive 'crease' aft of the cockpit section. So did **Matchbox** (Ref. No. 40203), but this brand was not famous for authenticity. Another **Mi-24D** kit was issued by **Esci/ERTL** (Ref. No. 9069); in this instance only the port cabin door can be opened. Alas, this model is inaccurate as well – the fuselage is 7 mm too short and Esci have got the wing anhedral wrong; also, the main rotor and the interior are too simplified. Mention has been made in web sources of a **Mi-24D** kit by an obscure company called **Plastic-SK**, but this may be a simple rebox. Again, **Alanger** offered a reboxed version of Heller's **Mi-24D** (Ref. No. 072018).

Now for the Mi-24V. Quite often the inscription on the box does not match what's inside. Take the **Italeri** kit (Ref. No. 014) released in 1992; the box art says 'Hind D' (Mi-24D) but actually the model represents the **Mi-24V**. Unfortunately the model suffers from serious inaccuracies, the most glaring one being the main rotor which turns in the wrong direction (anti-clockwise instead of clockwise) and is 10 mm too small in diameter, with too narrow blades. Other errors include a fuselage that's 6 mm too short, wings that are 6 mm too long in span, a tail rotor pylon with not enough sweepback and the wrong airfoil and so on. Nice features include crew entry doors that can be left open to show the cockpit interiors and the optional exhaust/air mixers. The decals are for a Soviet Mi-24V used in Afghanistan, a Czechoslovak Air Force example and a post-reunification German (Luftwaffe) example.

The Italeri Mi-24V has also been marketed under other brands: **Tamiya** (Ref. No. 60705, issued in 1993), **Revell** (Ref. No. 04417, issued in 1996, CzAF 'Tiger Meet' colours), **Zvezda** (Ref. No. 7213), **Bilek** (Ref. No. 922) and **Kitech** (aka **ZhengDefu**, Ref. No. 08M-M355 – a Chinese copy in *all* meanings). Here again is a case of mistaken identity: Zvezda has the box marked as 'Mi-24D', while Bilek's box art even shows a sharkmouthed CzAF Mi-24D! Incidentally, the Czech manufacturer also has a kit (Ref. No. 969) marketed as 'Mi-24D Hind V' (*sic*) but with a CzAF Mi-24V in NATO camouflage on the box top – though the sprues are identical.

Top to bottom: The box of Italeri's 1:72nd scale Mi-24V kit (with options to build a Mi-24D).

The Italeri Mi-24V built 'out of the box'.

Much effort is required to make the Italeri Mi-24V look realistic. This is an example of 'kit-bashing' – a much-modified Italeri Mi-24V in Ethiopian markings built by Gordon Zamit, using parts from the HobbyBoss kit.

The Italeri Mi-24V-cum-D has been reboxed under other brands, including Tamiya.

Hasegawa also has a **Mi-24V** kit. The current version (Ref. No. 00896) represents a Hungarian Air Force example in special colours.

The Chinese company **HobbyBoss** also has a **Mi-24V** kit (Ref. No. 87220). The box contains 215 parts (five grey plastic sprues and one clear); the proportions are reasonably accurate, with engraved panel lines and opening cabin doors, but the transparencies are poor. The kit includes parts to let you build a Mi-24D. The decals are for an Iraqi Mi-35 and a Russian Air Force helicopter used in Chechnya... which was really a *Mi-24P*, so the decals don't fit.

Fortunately, lately modellers have been treated to a decent all-new **Mi-24V/ Mi-24VP** kit by **Zvezda** (Ref. No. 7293), which is considered the most accurate 1:72nd scale *Hind* to date. The kit comprises 270 crisply moulded parts; the cabin and cockpit doors and engine/main gearbox cowlings can all be opened.

The **Mi-24P** was first offered by **Hasegawa** (Ref. No. 04021 or K-21) and then by **Italeri** (Ref. No. 024); of course, they share all the bugs of the respective Mi-24V kits. The latter kit is also available under

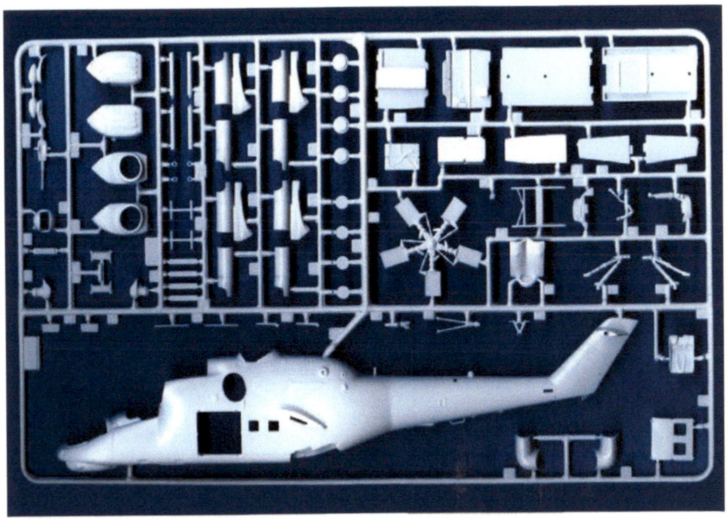

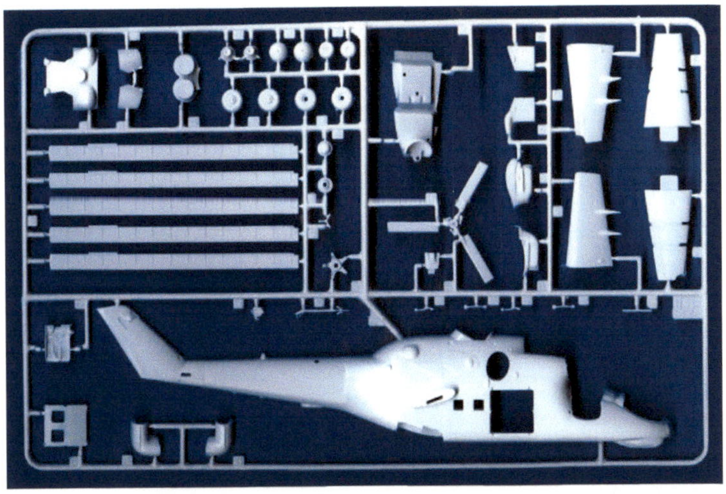

Top, upper and lower right: Revell's *Hind-D* kit is another iteration of Italeri offering a nice 'Tiger Meet' colour scheme.

Bottom left: The box of the 1:72nd scale Mi-24V kit (with options to build a Mi-24D).

Bottom right: The HobbyBoss Mi-24V partially assembled for a 'dry fit'.

Below: Bilek also marketed the Italeri Mi-24V/D under its own brand.

Above: The box of Zvezda's new 1:72nd scale Mi-24V/VP kit.

the **Zvezda** brand (Ref. No. 7212; oddly, the box top is marked 'Mi-24E' – a version that never existed) and **Kitech/ZhengDefu** (Ref. No. 08M-M354). Another **Mi-24P** kit was issued by **Esci/ERTL**; it is obviously based on their Mi-24D, with all its errors. The Canadian company **Hobbycraft** offers a **Mi-24P** kit (Ref. No. 2205) with a huge number of decal options, but the box art is suspiciously similar to Italeri's... another clone? **HobbyBoss** also has a **Mi-24P** kit based on their Mi-24V.

The most recent offering is the **Mi-35M** from **Zvezda** (Ref. No. 7276). It is based on their Mi-24V/VP but features new parts for the fixed landing gear, new clipped wings and new weapons. The model represents the black-painted prototype.

Right and below: The Zvezda Mi-24V built 'out of the box' by a modeller with the internet alias 'fsl'. The model was painted with Akan and Model Master paints.

Another Zvezda Mi-24V built by a modeller with the internet alias 'swordfish', using Tamiya paints.

Above left: Zvezda's new 1:72nd scale Mi-24V/VP has served as the basis for this Mi-35M kit.

Above right: The box of Italeri's 1:72nd scale Mi-24P kit.

Right and below: Italeri's Mi-24P has been reboxed by Zvezda. Here the Russian edition is seen as built 'out of the box' by a modeller with the internet alias 'kent', using Humbrol paints.

MIL' **Mi-24** 1:48th scale

Hinds to this scale are understandably few. **Monogram** offers a kit (Ref. No. 5819) that lets you build the **Mi-24D** or **Mi-24V**. As is often the case, the fuselage ended up being too short. The box contains 150 parts and a 20-page booklet with assembly instructions. The parts feature finely engraved panel lines, though the double rows of rivets near the fuselage mainframes are not reproduced; the cockpit doors and the starboard cabin door can be opened. Armament is limited to four UB-32A FFAR pods and two types of ATGMs; the decal sheet lets you build a Soviet example coded '27 Blue', East German Air Force Mi-24D '434' and a Luftwaffe machine serialled 96+50... which is a *Mi-24P* (oops!). The kit has been repackaged by **Revell** (Ref. No. 04462), with decals to build a Soviet Mi-24D/Mi-24V, a Czechoslovak Mi-24D, an Afghan Air Force Mi-25 (with late roundels) or a Nicaraguan Mi-25.

The Chinese company **MiniHobby Models** markets Ye Awfulle Pirate Copie of the Monogram kit (Ref. No. 80310); it is somewhat simplified and does not fit together as well as the original. However, they went that extra step and offer a kit of the **Mi-24P** (Ref. No. 80311) based on the former kit – which Monogram/Revell do not. These kits are often misidentified as produced by Trumpeter Models.

Above: The Monogram Mi-24V/D is also available under the Revell brand.

Top: The box of Monogram's 1:48th scale Mi-24V kit (with options to build a Mi-24D).

Above and left
The Monogram Mi-24V built 'out of the box' by 'kent'. The model was painted with Akan and Tamiya paints; Linden Hill decals were used.

MIL' Mi-24 1:35th scale

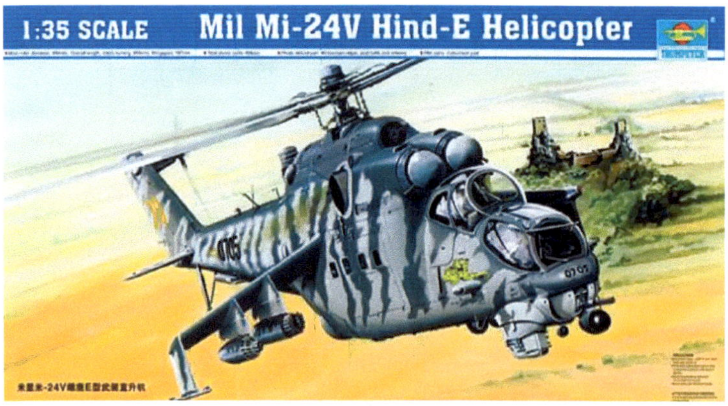

Above: The box of Trumpeter's 1:35th scale Mi-24V kit (with options to build a Mi-24D).

Don't ask us why the Chinese manufacturer **Trumpeter Models** chose to build the **Mi-24V** (Ref, No. 05103) to 1:35th scale (which is the standard for armour and military miniatures) rather than to one of the 'aviation standards' – say, 1:48th or 1:32nd. Released in 2003, this is the most detailed kit of the *Hind* to date. The box contains 12 grey plastic sprues (451 parts in all) and three clear sprues (18 parts) plus a PE plate (45 parts) and a piece of acetate film with two printed instrument panels, giving a total of 516 (!) parts. Moulding quality is good, with finely engraved panel lines and riveting, and few ejector pin marks in exposed areas that have to be dealt with. The cockpit and cabin doors (both) can be modelled open; so can the cowlings, revealing detailed engines. Curiously, the cowlings are in clear plastic with moulded internal detail, so the modeller may choose not to paint them, leaving the engines visible even if the cowlings are closed. Quite a large selection of weapons is

Right and below: Trumpeter's Mi-24V built by Sergey Budyanskiy. The model was improved, using the Eduard photo-etched parts set, and painted with Agama, Citadel, Revell and Tamiya paints.

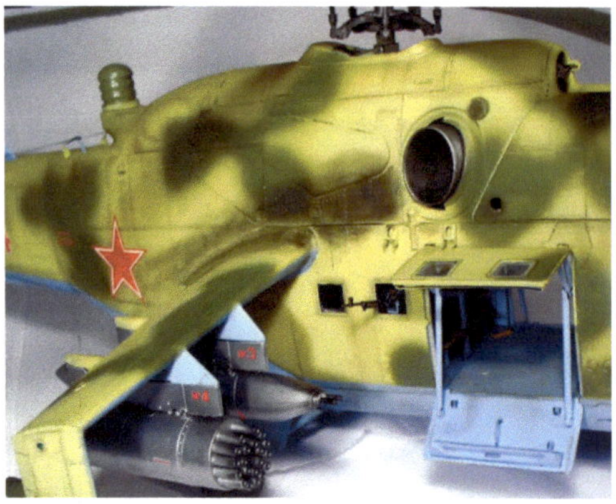

Right and opposite page: Trumpeter's Mi-24V built by a modeller with the internet alias 'sam-white'.

provided, including four 9M17P Falanga ATGMs and launch rails for same, which gives you the option of building the **Mi-24D**. Decals are provided for a Soviet Mi-24V stationed in East Germany and a Czech Air Force Mi-24V wearing a special 'tiger' colour scheme. The finished model is 56.5 cm long, with a rotor diameter of 49.4 cm and a wing span of 18.7 cm.

Though certainly impressive, this is a model for the seasoned hobbyist, and it has room for improvement for the super detailer. And yes, it does have its problems (hmm, was there *ever* a kit that didn't?). Though generally the kit comes together quite well, some areas, like the movable nose barbette and the wing/pylon joints, are tricky to assemble. The wing endplates come as separate parts and require care to position them correctly. Regrettably the model does not capture the Mi-24's distinctive 'lop-sided' appearance in head-on view due to the tilt of the powerplant/main gearbox assembly; but then, all other kit manufacturers doing the *Hind* have missed this point, too.

MIL' **Mi-24** 1:1000th scale

There are two **Mi-24D** kits on the market in this scale. **Revell** offers a kit that lets you build a Soviet or East German example (Ref. No. 04090), the finished model being 18.5 cm long, with a main rotor diameter of 17 cm. The other kit is by the South Korean manufacturer **Kangnam** (Ref. No. KGM7127) and is no longer available.

AFTERMARKET ITEMS

There are numerous items on the market for those who are not content with an 'out-of-the-box' *Hind*. In **1:72nd scale**, the Czech company **Eduard Models** offers a PE parts/transparency set for Hasegawa's Mi-24V/Mi-24P (also suitable for Italeri's kits) that lets you upgrade the cockpits, cabin, landing gear, rotor heads, machine-gun barbette, Raduga targeting system sensor pack, weapons pylons (including realistic launch rails for 9M17P Falanga ATGMs, should you want to build the Mi-24D) and UB-32A FFAR pods. Eduard also has a PE parts (exterior/interior/armament) and painting mask set (Ref. No. BIG7257) for the HobbyBoss kit. Similar PE sets for Hasegawa/ESCI/Italeri Mi-24D/Mi-24V kits are available from Ukrainian supplier **ACE** (Ref. No. 7209) and Polish supplier **Part** (Ref. Nos S72 003, S72 004 and S72 004B). Other useful accessories include a resin kit for the cockpits and cabin from the Czech company **Pavla Models**, weapons (such as FFAR pods) from the Russian company **VES** and resin/rubber wheels from the Russian company **Equipage**. **QuickBoost** offers the YakB-12,7 machine-gun and GSh-23L cannon in resin for the Zvezda Mi-24V/VP kit (Ref. No. 72316); **Heliborne** offers a **Mi-24R** conversion kit (Ref. No. 72006) with wingtip-mounted soil samplers, air sampler intake, bulged side window and so on in resin and clear plastic.

In **1:48th scale**, the **Cobra Company** offers several resin kits for the Monogram/Revell kit (the cockpit interiors and several sets of weapons, including more accurate Shtoorm ATGMs, B-8V20 FFAR pods, UPK-23-250 cannon pods, KMGU-2 submunitions pods and the like. The Czech company **CMK Kits** has three resin kits for the same kit – two exterior parts kits (Ref. No. 4081 and 4138), which include drop tanks, flare dispensers, improved stabilisers, Raduga sensor pack and wheels, and a 'plug' for the tailboom allowing you to rectify the shortfall in length, and a weapons kit (Ref. No. 4080) that lets you build the **Mi-24P**. **Eduard Models** offers a PE exterior parts kit for the Monogram/Revell kit (Ref. No. 48266); so does **Part** (Ref. Nos. S48 003 and S48 004), while **Pavla Models** offers several resin kits for the same product – cockpit interiors (Ref. No. D48008), wheels (Ref. No. D48012), flare dispensers (Ref. No. D48013). As it does in 1:72nd scale, **Heliborne** offers a **Mi-24R** conversion kit (Ref. No. 48006), but in greater detail.

Trumpeter's **1:35th scale** kit is not left out either. The US military resin accessory kits manufacturer **Verlinden Productions** (Ref. No. VL-2349) offers a cockpit/cabin parts set; **Eduard Models** has a PE parts and painting mask set (Ref. No. BIG3226) and a pre-painted instrument panel set (Ref. No. 32521). **Scale Aircraft Conversions** offers a set of stronger landing gear struts cast in white metal (Ref. No. 35001), while **Profimodeller** has a small PE parts set for the wheel discs (Ref. No. 32055).

Mi-24V '07 Yellow' of the Russian Ministry of the Interior (MoI) operating in Chechnya in 2003 during the Second Chechen War. The vertical white stripe on the tailboom is an insignia of MoI Interior Troops helicopters.

Mi-24V '03 Yellow' of the Russian MoI Interior Troops operating from Khankala AB near Groznyy, Chechnya, in 2007. Note the non-standard uniform green camouflage on the upper surfaces.

Mi-24V '24 White' of the Russian peacekeeping forces in Georgia in the 2000s.

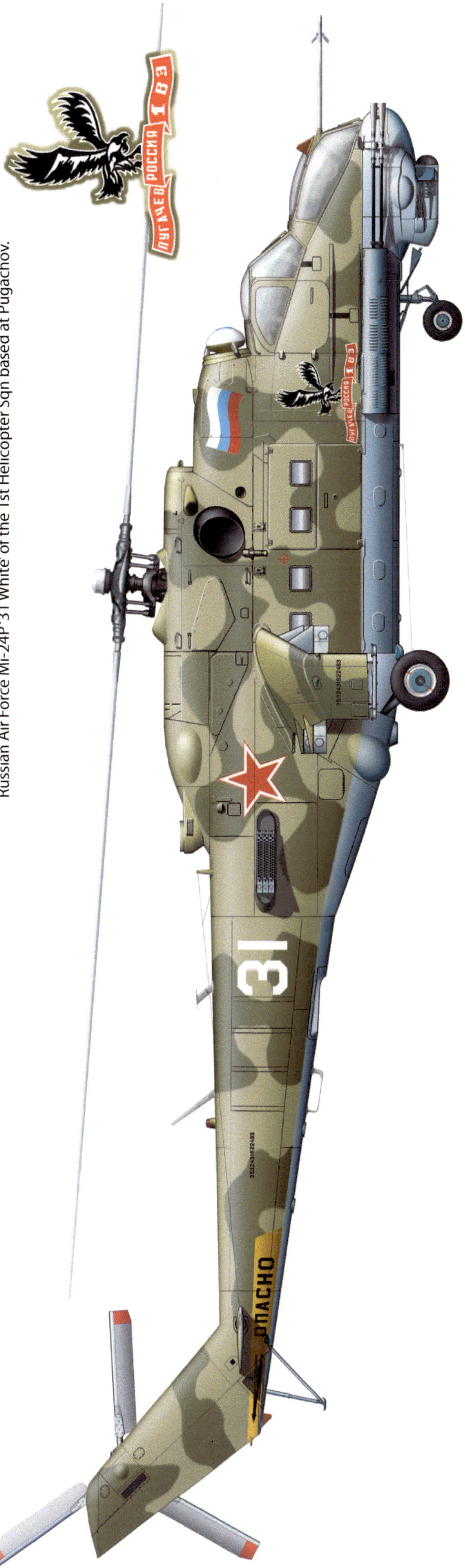

Russian Air Force Mi-24P '31 White' of the 1st Helicopter Sqn based at Pugachov.

A Russian Air Force Mi-24P seconded to the UN Peace Forces contingent in Kosovo (KFOR), Prishtina-Slatina airport. Note the overpainted Russian stars and the KFOR chevron replacing the tactical code.

Russian Navy Mi-24VP '31 Red' of the Baltic Fleet/125th Independent Helicopter Sqn, Chernyakhovsk, February 2007.

Mi-24VP '40 Red' of the Baltic Fleet/125th Independent Helicopter Sqn, Chernyakhovsk, September 2006; note the Russian Navy flag on the cowling.

Mi-24P '15 Yellow' of the 344th Combat Training & Aircrew conversion Centre at Torzhok was one of several wearing the striking livery of the Berkuty (Golden Eagles) display team. Note the Russian Air Force tri-colour insignia applied correctly, with a narrow blue outline around the red star.

Russian Air Force Mi-24P '37 White' operated by the military pilot college at Syzran'. Note the tri-colour star insignia with an excessively wide blue edging in the wrong shade of blue.

Russian Air Force Mi-35M '56 Yellow'/RF- in the new all-grey colour scheme, 2012.

Mil' Mi-28

The Russian Apache

The combat helicopter concept underwent numerous changes in the course of its gestation. One of the basic problems consisted in formulating the most effective tactics of the attack helicopter's operational use, the appropriate armament and, consequently, the machine's basic layout and structural design. In parallel with the transport/ assault helicopter concept embodied in the Mi-24, Mikhail L. Mil' and his associates conceived a project of a dedicated highly manoeuvrable rotary-wing 'flying tank' serving as a platform for all possible kinds of armament; the carriage of troops was no longer envisaged. A marked interest in this kind of rotorcraft was in no small degree due to the fact that the Lockheed Corporation had built a fast and agile combat helicopter – the widely publicised AH-56A Cheyenne (which never reached production, though). In an attempt to attain high performance comparable to that of fixed-wing attack aircraft, the AH-56A was provided with a pusher propeller, stub wings, a rigid bearingless main rotor and a complex navigation/attack suite.

The Communist Party Central Committee/Council of Ministers directive of 6th May 1968 formally launching the Mi-24 programme contained a clause that the Mi-24 would serve as basis for an advanced attack helicopter possessing greater speed and good stability and manoeuvrability. By the end of the year the preliminary design department of the Mil' OKB prepared the first project of the Mi-28 – a compound helicopter based on the Mi-24 but without the troop cabin and with a rigid main rotor, additional means of forward propulsion and heavier armament. Unfortunately the military had no clear idea as to what this machine should look like, and the firm was overburdened with current projects; this, together with the illness and demise of Mikhail L. Mil', prevented the concept from being put into practice immediately.

The Mi-28 compound helicopter project was revived under the OKB's new head Marat N. Tischenko in 1972 when a similar AAH (Army Attack Helicopter) programme was going full steam ahead in the USA. By then the Soviet Air Force command had formulated its operational requirements. The compound helicopter was to provide CAS, destroy armoured vehicles, escort troopship helicopters during assault operations and wage war against low-speed aerial targets, such as helicopters. The main armament was to comprise up to eight 9M114 Shtoorm ATGMs and a 30-mm movable cannon; the total warload was estimated at 1,200 kg (2,650 lb). The helicopter had a crew of two (pilot and WSO); the cockpits and vital items were to feature armour plating affording protection against 12.7-mm (.50 calibre) machine-gun fire. The flight/navigation suite was to ensure round-the-clock all-weather operation. A maximum speed of 380-420 km/h (236 to 261 mph) was envisaged.

The customer specified that the Mi-28 be provided with devices allowing the crew to bail out in an emergency. Ejection seats were the first choice; however, you obviously cannot eject through the rotor disc. Flight tests conducted earlier by the Mil' OKB had shown that it was difficult to ensure safe separation of the rotor blades by jettisoning them; therefore the designers opted for a side-by-side twin-rotor layout which not only permitted safe ejection outside the rotor disc area but also made it possible to incorporate wings offloading the rotors. A project along these lines was prepared in 1973. The machine was to have a maximum take-off weight of 11.5 tonnes (25,360 lb) and be powered by two 2,800-shp Izotov TV3-117F turboshafts; the twin rotors of 10.3 m (33 ft 9³³⁄₆₄ in) diameter were augmented by a pusher propeller aft of the tail unit. A full-size mock-up was built, but in the mid-1970s the customer revised the concept of combat helicopter operations. Combat at relatively high altitudes and speeds emulating the tactics of fixed-wing attack aircraft gave way to low-level operations involving nap-of-the-earth (NOE) flying; this was expected to ensure high battlefield survivability. Hence in the early 1970s the Mil' OKB prepared, at its own initiative, several draft projects of combat helicopters with additional propulsive devices. They included a single-rotor helicopter with a main rotor of 16 m (52 ft 6 in) in diameter and two TV3-117F engines; this variant was deemed to be the most promising for the Mi-28. Relinquishing the compound helicopter layout gave a substantial improvement in the payload/weight ratio and the weapon load; also, the structure was simplified.

Emphasis on low-altitude operations made it possible to dispense with the crew ejection system. Studies showed that in the event of a helicopter being shot down at low altitude the crew had no time to bail out and had to rely on crash survival features. At the time a concept emerged of using crashwor-

As originally envisaged, the Mi-28 was to have been a compound helicopter with side-by-side rotors. Note the pusher propeller and the ventrally mounted cannon.

thy structural elements that could sustain deformations with a high safety margin, crashworthy undercarriage and seats; this meant that ejection would no longer be absolutely necessary to ensure crew survival in a shootdown. Proceeding from this, the OKB opted for the classic single-rotor layout offering the advantage of structural simplicity. The helicopter was to be powered by a modified version of the powerful and reliable TV3-117 engines which were well mastered in production.

Concurrently the designers discussed the requirements concerning the armament, the navigation/attack suite and other equipment; methods were evolved for determining ways of enhancing combat survivability and reducing the helicopter's visual, heat and noise signature. This work was conducted in specialised research, design and test organisations; the most prominent among these were TsAGI (Central Aero- & Hydrodynamics Institute), LII (Flight Research Institute), VIAM (All-Union Research Institute for Aviation Materials), GosNIIAS (State Research Institute for Aviation Systems), GNIKI VVS (Red Banner State Research Institute of the Air Force), RPKB (Ramenskoye Avionics Design Bureau) and others. A steadily growing number of institutions representing the customer, the defence industry, electronics industry and other branches were involved in the development of the future combat helicopter's navigation/attack suite. Gradually the Mi-28 project was transformed into a national programme comparable in its complexity with the construction of an advanced combat aircraft.

By 1976 the main features of the Mi-28's outlook had been finalised. The project work was supervised by Deputy Chief Designer A. N. Ivanov; Marat N. Weinberg was appointed chief project engineer. The technical proposal evolved in the Mil' OKB was positively assessed by the customer.

Concurrently, the rival Kamov OKB submitted their V-80 combat helicopter project (later redesignated Ka-50). This utilised Kamov's traditional coaxial twin-rotor layout; proceeding from the experience of shipboard helicopter operations, the Kamov OKB came to the conclusion that helicopters featuring this layout would also prove effective in the CAS role. The V-80 was unique among attack helicopters in being a single-seater; the functions of the WSO would largely be performed by the automated avionics suite. On 16th December 1976 the Communist Party Central Committee and the Council of Ministers issued a directive calling for the development of both helicopters on a competitive basis. Since no clear-cut specification had been issued by the Air Force, the Mil' and Kamov designers enjoyed carte blanche as regards the design concept, and then tried to convince the customer of the viability of their concepts. As a result, the two firms began designing machines of a totally different class differing in aerodynamic configuration, take-off weight, crew complement, armament, equipment and the like. As distinct from the V-80 which had no analogues, the Mi-28 was designed in accordance with the battle-proven concept of a two-crew combat helicopter based on a clear-cut division of functions between the crew members.

As reference points the Mil' OKB took the Mi-24 and the best foreign helicopter in the class – the Hughes (later McDonnell Douglas Helicopters, now Boeing) AH-64 Apache which they aspired to surpass on all major counts. The designers strove to achieve high weight efficiency coupled with the requisite strength, reliability and resistance to battle damage. Numerous structural layout versions were considered, including an unorthodox fuselage configuration featuring a so-called 'central core' where all vital parts and systems were placed inside a central longitudinal stressed structure flanked by equipment bays and assemblies of secondary importance. However, calculations showed it would be difficult to achieve the necessary strength and vibration characteristics; besides, the equipment would be too vulnerable. The attractive configuration had to be relinquished in favour of a conventional semi-monocoque fuselage.

To ensure survivability, systems components were duplicated and placed far apart or located in such a way that vital units were protected by less important ones; the same purpose was served by armour-plating arrangements, structural materials and dimensions of structural members carefully chosen in such a way as to exclude catastrophic structural failure in case of battle damage for long enough to allow the chopper to return home. The all-round bulletproof glazing could withstand hits of 12.7-mm armour-piercing bullets and 20-mm high-explosive/fragmentation cannon shells; the main rotor blades were designed to survive hits of 30-mm rounds.

The cockpit layout became a key element of the design. Side-by-side seating was rejected outright because this layout did not afford the necessary field of view for either crewmember and complicated bailing out in an emergency. The engineers opted for a stepped-tandem arrangement which had proved its worth on the Mi-24, with the pilot sitting behind and above the WSO; the individual cockpits had car-type doors.

By the end of 1977 the OKB had completed the advanced development project (ADP) and reached an understanding with the subcontractors responsible for the equipment and armament. The subsequent eighteen months were used for co-ordinating with the customer all aspects of the specification concerning the helicopter and its avionics and armament fit, and in 1979 the OKB started detail design of the helicopter and the testing of the first experimental specimens of assemblies and systems.

In its final form the **Mi-28** (*izdeliye* 280) had a narrow fuselage mated to a low-set slender tailboom terminating in a swept tail rotor pylon with a portside stabiliser at the top. The low location of the tailboom precluded the possibility of the main rotor blades striking it during a violent manoeuvre. Like its predecessor, the Mi-28 had anhedral stub wings with four pylons for carrying external stores; however, the wings had much shorter span (4.88 m; 16 ft 0⅛ in) and lacked vertical endplates. The stub wings could be jettisoned in an emergency. The helicopter had a number of built-in survivability features. For example, the powerplant was basically the same as on the Mi-24 – two TV3-117VM turboshafts plus an AI-9V APU; however, the engines were installed on the fuselage sides above the wing roots (rather than side by side on top of the fuselage), eliminating the risk of them being disabled by a single hit, and the exhaust/air mixers reducing the helicopter's IR signature were permanently installed. The TV3-117VM was rated at 1,950 shp, enabling the helicopter to fly with one engine inoperative. The lateral installation of the engines necessitated the use of bevel gearboxes transmitting the torque to the main gearbox. The air intakes were provided with vortex-type dust filters. A water injection system ensured surge-free running of the engines when unguided rockets were launched.

The Mi-28 had a five-blade main rotor, which featured a radically new elastomeric hub, and a four-blade tail rotor featuring a squashed-X layout for noise attenuation and higher efficiency. For the first time in Soviet helicopter design practice the Mi-28 made use of maintenance-free rotor hubs requiring no regular lubrication. The rotor blades were of composite construction with a honeycomb filler in both cases. Unfortunately, the development of the X-shaped tail rotor took longer than expected, and early Mi-28 prototypes flew with stock Mi-24 tail rotors until 1987.

A peculiarity of the Mi-28 was the fixed tailwheel undercarriage with trailing-arm

Another project version of the Mi-28 that was closer to the end result – a conventional helicopter with a strong family resemblance to the Mi-24. Judging by the consecutive 'tactical codes', the two mock-ups were built concurrently.

main units. This layout was dictated by the need to fit the machine's overall dimensions into certain limits, making it airliftable; the main units made it possible to reduce the helicopter's ground clearance and overall height before loading into an aircraft.

The Mi-28 was provided with an avionics suite permitting round-the-clock/all-weather operations. The helicopter's mission equipment comprised the KOPS combined surveillance/targeting system in an under-nose turret (used by the navigator/WSO for detecting, identifying and monitoring the target during missile launches and gunnery), the PrPNK-28 flight/navigation/attack suite, and a helmet-mounted sight (HMS) for the pilot allowing him to aim the cannon. The PrPNK-28 was developed by RPKB; it enabled detection and identification of targets, accurate aiming of the cannon and unguided weapons. It also improved the helicopter's handling, allowing it to follow a predesignated course and hover stably over a designated point, and determined the helicopter's location continuously. The system comprised primary data sensors, two onboard computers and control and display devices. The sensors included data systems for the vertical parameters, flight direction, altitude and speed, a Doppler speed and drift indicator Control and indication devices included: an automatic map, navigation instruments and a data presentation system.

The armament of the Mi-28 comprised a permanently installed NPPU-28 turret under the nose mounting a 30-mm (1.18-in) 2A42 cannon, as well as guided and unguided weapons carried on the stub wing pylons. Developed by the Tula instrument design bureau (TKB), the 2A42 cannon was borrowed from the Soviet Army's BMP-2 infantry fighting vehicle; it was a selectable-feed cannon firing armour-piercing and high-explosive/fragmentation rounds. The cannon could be traversed and elevated within wide angles; this allowed the crew to fire simultaneously on two targets located at different azimuths. The ammunition supply was placed in two cases flanking the breech of the cannon; this enhanced the weapon's reliability and the helicopter's survivability. Guided weapons comprised up to sixteen 9M120 Ataka-V or 9M114 Shturm-V supersonic ATGMs (with radio command guidance) developed by the Kolomna Machinery Design Bureau; these were carried on special four-pack adapters and intended for destroying not only ground targets but also low- and slow-flying aircraft. unguided armament that could be carried on inboard underwing racks included B-5V35, B-8V20 or B-13L1 FFAR pods with rockets, GUV pods (housing either three Gatling machine guns or a grenade launcher), and KMGU-2 submunitions dispensers. The underwing racks could also be used for carrying 250- and 500-kg (551- and 1,102-lb) bombs or auxiliary fuel tanks. Later the arsenal of the Mi-28 was supplemented by S-24B heavy unguided rockets, UPK-23-250 cannon pods and ZB-500 napalm containers.

For self-protection the Mi-28 was equipped with active electronic countermeasures and IRCM equipment, a radar homing and warning system (RHAWS) and a laser warning system alerting the crew that the helicopter was being 'painted' by enemy radars or laser target designators, and IRCM flare dispensers for protection against heat-seeking missiles.

Placing the heaviest assemblies and systems close to the CG enhanced the Mi-28's manoeuvrability. Mil' OKB engineers placed considerable emphasis on ease of maintenance in the field, making all systems and equipment readily accessible; compared to the Mi-24, approximately three times fewer maintenance man-hours were required. A peculiarity of the Mi-28 was that a lot of free space remained in the centre fuselage equipment bay, which allowed it to be used as a cargo hold (for transporting ground support equipment during redeployment to a new base) or for evacuating the crew of another helicopter.

Different configurations were tried when designing the various units of the Mi-28. In particular, the Mil' OKB designed and built an alternative and equally new torsion-bar hub (which was rejected eventually); a transmission shaft made of carbonfibre reinforced plastic was also developed. The selection of the optimum design features was accompanied by comprehensive tests of assemblies with the use of test rigs, of which no fewer than 54 were built. To conduct preliminary flight testing of the Mi-28's rotor system, engines, autopilot, navigation/attack suite and guided missiles the OKB converted four Mi-24 helicopters and several Mi-8s into flying testbeds.

Together with their colleagues from specialised R&D establishments, Mil' OKB designers conducted extensive research to ensure high combat survivability and a low heat signature. These included ballistic tests of the cockpits, fuel tank, main and tail rotor blades, transmission shaft, control linkage and hydraulic system; the results of this research made it possible to optimise the armour plating, which consisted of ceramic plates bonded to the forward fuselage structure. For the first time in Soviet helicopter design practice the Mi-28's heat signature at all aspects was determined experimentally.

A large scope of research was undertaken in a joint effort to create a passive crash protection system for the helicopter's crew (extra shock absorbers in the undercarriage, movable cockpit floor etc.). This ensured that the G loads affecting the crew were reduced to physiologically acceptable levels in the event of a crash landing with a sink rate of up to 12 m/sec (39.37 ft/sec). The mechanisms actuating the system were located on the main gear units' shock absorbers. They caused the crashworthy crew seats to travel 30 cm (about 1 ft) downwards, protecting the crew from excessive

'012 Yellow', the first prototype Mi-28. Note the braced temporary air data probe attached to the cannon (which has lateral ammunition boxes) and the 'glasshouse' enclosing the targeting system turret.

G loads, and moved the cyclic pitch stick forward to prevent injuries to the pilot. The harness system ensured that the shoulder straps were tightened automatically in an emergency situation, preventing injuries.

In August 1980, taking note of the progress in the development of the Mi-28, the VPK authorised the construction of two prototypes without waiting for the official approval of the final mock-up. The Air Force's mock-up review commission passed its positive verdict only at the end of 1981, when the static test airframe was already complete and the first prototype was in mid-assembly. Therefore the first prototype completed in July 1982 was brought up to the required standard in the process of development and flight testing.

The Mi-28 was intended for detecting and destroying enemy armoured vehicles and personnel in localities with even and hilly/mountainous terrain, as well as low-speed aerial targets within visual range in good and moderately adverse weather. The helicopter's dimensions allowed it to be air-lifted by the Il'yushin IL-76 *Candid* heavy

The first prototype in flight. Note the dorsally located exhaust/air mixer scoops.

'022 Yellow', the second prototype Mi-28, with weapons under the starboard wing and test equipment pods under the port wing. Note the revised targeting system turret. The first two Mi-28s had three-blade tail rotors.

transport without dismantling. The design of the main assemblies and systems enabled the helicopter to operate off-base from unprepared pads over the course of 15 days.

On 10th November 1982 the Mi-28 made its first hover at the hands of project test pilot Gurghen R. Karapetyan and navigator V. V. Tsygankov lifted; the first free flight followed on 19th December. The very next day the helicopter was officially submitted for the first stage of the flyoff against the V-80; this was successfully completed in 1984, and the helicopter was transferred to GNIKI VVS for the second stage of the flyoff. Being intended primarily for performance/handling tests, the first prototype lacked armament and mission avionics. These were fitted to the second prototype completed in September 1983 and incorporating the changes requested by the mock-up review commission. At the end of the year the second prototype underwent live weapons trials.

By 1986 the Mi-28 prototype met all the specified performance characteristics and even surpassed them on some counts. The only wish expressed by the customer boiled down to widening the G limits, since the helicopter's control system permitted it to manoeuvre with higher G loads. As a result, the permissible G load during a stall turn reached 2.65 at the altitude of 500 m (1,640 ft) and 1.8 at 4,000 m (13,120 ft). The maximum speeds of sideways and tail-first flight were also considerably increased. All development work on the helicopter's specialised systems and weapons integration was completed on the second prototype during 1986. When the intended X-shaped tail rotor was introduced in 1987, the Mi-28's appearance and equipment complement could be regarded as finalised.

Impressed by the results of the Mi-28's initial trials, the Ministry of Aircraft Industry ordered the helicopter into production at the Arsen'yev aircraft plant in February 1984. Had everything gone as planned, the Soviet Air Force could have taken delivery of its first Mi-28s as early as 1987, yet this prospect failed to materialise. Even though American research had shown the impossibility of cre-

'032 Yellow', the third prototype, was the first Mi-28A. Here the helicopter is shown in its original camouflage with a Le Bourget exhibit code on the tailboom. The new four-blade squashed-X tail rotor and revised exhaust/air mixers are clearly visible here.

ating a fully-capable single-seat combat helicopter (given the US state of the art in electronics), Soviet military specialists arrived at the opposite conclusion – they considered that Soviet avionics houses were capable of developing an automated suite allowing a single-seat helicopter to operate successfully at ultra-low altitudes. In 1984 the Air Force made its choice, selecting the V-80 helicopter for further development and production in Arsen'yev as the Ka-50. Around the same time the western intelligence community got wind of the Mi-28's existence and the helicopter was assigned the NATO reporting name *Havoc*.

In April 1986 the Mi-28 and the V-80 underwent simultaneous tests at the Gorokhovets target range; the Mi-28 emerged as the winner, detecting and 'destroying' 25 targets out of 25 and escaping detection by the 'adversary'. Nevertheless, without waiting for the completion of the flyoff, the military came to the conclusion that the Ka-50 *'has great development potential and entails lesser expenses for setting up and maintaining an operational unit'*. To enhance the Ka-50's efficiency, the military suggested target designation via data link from a special reconnaissance helicopter or forward air controllers on the ground; yet such a helicopter was yet to be built and the Ka-50's avionics and armament were still troublesome. Therefore, no one took the risk of terminating the Mi-28 programme, only the funding was reduced. Despite this, the Mi-28 successfully completed State acceptance trials and proved its efficiency. Taking these positive results into account, on 14th December 1987 the Communist Party Central Committee and the Council of Ministers issued a directive ordering the Mi-28 into production at the Rostov Helicopter Plant.

Here we have to go back a bit. In 1985 the Mil' OKB had begun construction of the third Mi-28 prototype incorporating all the changes requested by the customer and the updates introduced by then. In 1987 the updated helicopter was designated **Mi-28A** (*izdeliye* 286). It was powered by uprated 2,225-shp TV3-117VMA engines optimised for high-altitude operations; additionally, it featured improved avionics, revised exhaust suppressors and a modified main gearbox. The Mi-28A introduced wingtip-mounted pods housing IRCM flare dispensers and ESM equipment. The NATO reporting name was *Havoc-A*.

Tests of the Mi-28A began in January 1988. In 1989 the helicopter made its international debut at the 38th Paris Air Show and at the helicopter exhibition in Redhill near London. That same year the Mi-28 was officially unveiled to the public in its home country during the annual Aviation Day display. In January 1991 a second Mi-28A development aircraft joined the test programme. In September 1993 the helicopters brilliantly demonstrated their performance and superiority over the Ka-50 in the course of an army exercise. The expediency of the two-seat layout became obvious to everyone. In 1993, when the first stage of the State trials was completed, the Russian military issued a preliminary assessment calling for

The same helicopter in the late 1990s in new colours as '032 White outline' with bear's head artwork on the engine cowlings. Note the full weapons load – eight 9M120 ATGMs and two B-8V20 FFAR pods.

Head-on view of the fourth prototype, '042 Yellow', during 'hot-and-high' trials.

the manufacture of a pre-production batch. The Rostvertol Helicopter Production Association started gearing up for series production, and construction of the first production Mi-28A funded by the enterprise's own means began in 1994.

The Mi-28A was rated very highly by specialists both at home and abroad. It fully met its mission requirements and was superior on many counts to other helicopters in its class; its handling and agility ensured a high degree of survivability in air-to-air combat. The armed forces of many nations took an interest in the *Havoc*. In the autumn of 1990 Iraq ordered the type and signed an agreement with Russia on joint production of the **Mi-28L** (*litsenzi**on**nyy* – licence-built); however, the First Gulf War foiled these plans. In the autumn of 1995 the Swedish Ministry of Defence shortlisted the Mi-28A and the Boeing AH-64 Apache in a tender for a new combat helicopter. The Russian rotorcraft fulfilled the entire test programme, including live weapons tests, and showed itself as 'very reliable and well suited for field conditions'; the only demand addressed to it called for the addition of systems giving night capability.

Meanwhile, Russian Air Force test pilots started mastering the Mi-28A. However, the work proceeded at a slow pace due to funding shortfalls, and the helicopter's equipment was growing obsolescent. Hence the new General Designer Marat N. Weinberg decided (with the customer's consent) to abandon the Mi-28A at the concluding stage of the trials and concentrate all efforts on the development of the **Mi-28N** (*noch**noy*** – night-capable) version suited for round-the-clock/all-weather operations with a radically new fifth-generation integrated avionics suite. The Mi-28N is regarded as the Russian answer to the advent of the AH-64D Apache Longbow equipped with a mast-mounted radar (MMR). The reporting name is *Havoc-B*.

Bearing in mind that the Mi-28's basic design, armament and protection systems fully met current requirements, it was

Another aspect of the same machine with a Le Bourget exhibit code on the tailboom. Note the wingtip ESM/IRCM pods.

decided to develop only new avionics incorporating state-of-the-art electronic components, and a new VR-29 main gearbox (the original VR-28 gearbox was incompatible with an MMR). In early 1993 the customer's commission inspected the mock-up and the ADP was approved, whereupon design work on the Mi-28N began.

The integrated avionics suite of the Mi-28N was to ensure NOE flying in manual and automatic mode making use of map information and 3-D synthesised imaging of the locality; detection and identification of targets; concerted action with automatic target distribution between helicopters in a group; two-way data exchange between helicopters and airborne or ground command posts. It comprised the WSO's stabilised surveillance/targeting system with optical, IR and TV channels; the pilot's thermal imager and laser rangefinder; a helmet-mounted target designation/indication system and the pilot's NVG; a data presentation system with liquid-crystal colour displays; inertial and satellite navigation systems, as well as a geomagnetic navigation system; a communications suite; and an MMR with a 360° field of view. The radar allows the helicopter to search for ground and airborne targets while hiding behind obstacles; it also caters for piloting and navigation tasks. The weapons range was augmented by 9M39 Igla (Needle) IR-homing supersonic air-to-air missiles.

The first prototype Mi-28N was rolled out on 16th August 1996, performing its first flight on 14th November that year at the hands of test pilot V. V. Yoodin and navigator S. V. Nikulin. It featured a restyled nose with two completely new targeting system turrets. Manufacturer's flight tests began on 30th April 1997 but were hampered by an acute shortage of funding caused by Russia's eco-

The first prototype of the night-capable Mi-28N, '014 White outline', taxies during its official unveiling for the press.

Mi-28N '014 White outline' at the Mil' flight test facility. The 'cheek pouches' housing avionics, the totally different chin-mounted optoelectronic system turrets and the mast-mounted radar 'egg' are clearly visible.

nomic and political crisis. A change of government in 1998, with a resulting increase in defence spending, brought a change of fortune for the Mi-28N; still, it was not until March 2004 that the second prototype was completed at the Rostvertol plant. In January 2005 it was flown to Moscow to complete manufacturer's tests, and in May 2005 the helicopter was submitted for State acceptance trials. That same year Army

Above: The first prototype Mi-28N at the hover. Note the Russian flag superimposed on the star; this was one of the rejected versions of the Russian Air Force's new insignia.

Left and below: Two aspects of the second prototype Mi-28N, '024 Yellow', at Zhukovskiy. Note the much neater radome and the absence of the cheek fairings seen on the first machine.

Opposite page: Mi-28N '024 Yellow' performs a flight at Zhukovskiy.

024

Right: Boresighting the 2A42 cannon of Mi-28N '024 Yellow' at a test range.

Opposite page: Mi-28N '02 Yellow' at the Rostvertol factory airfield (Rostov-Severnyy).

Gen. Yuriy Baluyevskiy, the Russian Armed Forces' Chief of General Staff, announced that the Mi-28N, which by then had received the popular name *Noch**noy** o**khot**nik* (Night Hunter), would be Russian Army Aviation's principal combat helicopter, whereas the Ka-50 and its two-seat derivative, the Ka-52, would be used by the Special Forces. Also in 2005, the Russian MoD placed an order for an initial 67 Mi-28Ns, with deliveries due for completion in 2013; Russia's overall requirement for the type is estimated at 300.

The first pre-production example took to the air at Rostov-Severnyy airfield at the end of 2005; low-rate initial production started in 2006. The pre-production batch of *Havocs* (still minus the mast-mounted radar and wingtip IRCM/ESM pods) was delivered to the Russian Army Aviation's 344th Combat Training & Aircrew Conversion Centre in Torzhok. Production Mi-28Ns are powered by Klimov VK-2500-02 engines with a take-off rating of 2,000/2,200/2,400 shp (depending on control system settings) and a 2,700-shp contingency rating; thy are equipped with the Tor (Torus – or Thor, if you like) missile guidance system and the GOES-521 gyrostabilised optoelectronic surveillance/targeting system developed by UOMZ.

The Mi-28N had its 'baptism of fire' in June 2006 when two development aircraft took part in the joint Russian/Belarussian Exercise *Shchit So**yoo**za-2006* (Union Shield 2006). In September 2007 the military assessed the results of Stage A of the State acceptance trials and revised the operational requirement as regards mission equipment. On 22nd January 2008 the Torzhok training centre took delivery of the first two full-scale production machines (again minus MMR). Stage B of the trials was completed on 26th December that year; on 15th October 2009 the Mi-28N was officially included into the Russian Air Force inventory. Thus, justice had been done.

The 387th Army Aviation Base (formerly 487th Independent Helicopter Regiment) at Budyonnovsk, Stavropol' Area (North Caucasian Military District), became the first operational unit to field the *Havoc* in 2009, relinquishing its Mi-24Ps. The 393rd AvB (formerly 55th IHR) at Korenovsk, also in the Stavropol' Area, followed suit in October 2010. Overall, deliveries in 2009-10 amounted to 38 production *Havocs*; that year the Russian MoD followed up with a second order for 30 Mi-28Ns to be delivered by 2015.

Generally the Mi-28N surpasses by far the obsolete Mi-24V/Mi-24P (though not the much-improved Mi-35M). Many operations are automated, particularly those associated with weapons aiming and guidance. The helicopter is nimble but also stable in headwinds and crosswinds.

Unfortunately one Mi-28N has been lost in a fatal crash on 15th February 2011 caused by engine failure at low altitude. Before that, another Mi-28N had a similar mishap on 19th June 2009 when the engines surged after ingesting blast gases at the hover; on that occasion the crew walked away and the machine was eventually rebuilt.

In 2012 the Mil' Company began trials of the Mi-28N in its intended configuration with the N025 *Arba**let*** (Crossbow) MMR in a spherical radome. Other versions currently under development are the **Mi-28NM** (*moderni**zee**rovannyy* – upgraded) offering enhanced flight performance, combat efficiency and survivability; the **Mi-28UB** dual-control version (*oo**cheb**no-boye**voy** [verto**lyot**]* – combat trainer); and the **Mi-28NE** export version. The prototype of the latter was demonstrated to the Algerian Air Force in 2008; in 2011 the Mi-28NE was entered (unsuccessfully) in an Indian Air Force tender for a new combat helicopter.

02

02

Right: '35 Yellow', a pre-production Mi-28N operated by the 344th Combat Training & Aircrew conversion Centre at Torzhok, with B-13L FFAR pods. The first production *Havoc-Bs* had this two-tone camouflage scheme.

Above: '32 Yellow', the first pre-production Mi-28N, fires S-13 heavy FFARs during trials.

Right: Pre-production and initial production Mi-28Ns (exemplified by '41 Yellow') lacked the mast-mounted radar and even the wingtip pods. Note the 'Russian Air Force' titles.

Left: The final assembly shop at Rostvertol, with two initial production Mi-28Ns in the foreground; note the open cockpit doors. Two Russian Air Force Mi-24Ps undergoing refurbishment are visible beyond, with new-build Mi-35Ms and Mi-26 heavy-lift helicopters in the background.

Above: An initial production Mi-28N ('42 Yellow') from Torzhok carrying two drop tanks.

Left: A line-up of blue-coded Mi-28Ns from the 387th Army Aviation Base at Budyonnovsk – the Russian Air Force's first operational unit to fly the type.

Above: Five 344th Combat Training & Aircrew Conversion Centre Mi-28Ns at Torzhok with a Mi-8MTV (foreground), Mi-8MTV-5 and Ka-50 in the background.

Left: 'Toad's eye view' of a 387th Army Aviation Base Mi-28N showing details of the targeting system turrets, the cannon installation and the sturdy landing gear.

Below: 387th AvB Mi-28Ns '02 Blue' and '05 Blue' in formation. The latter was lost in a fatal crash on 15th February 2011.

Opposite, top: Six Mi-28Ns with drop tanks fly over Moscow in delta formation on 9th May 2010 during the Victory Day celebrations.

Opposite, bottom: Two Mi-28Ns in the current overall grey scheme ('03 Yellow'/RF-93275 and '50 Yellow'/RF-) makes a demo flight at Zhukovskiy during the Russian Air Force centennial celebrations in August 2012.

50
03

THE Mi-28 IN DETAIL

The following brief description applies to the Mi-28N.

The fuselage is built in four sections (forward and centre sections, tailboom and tail rotor pylon) and is made of aluminium alloy and composites. The *forward fuselage* incorporates two cockpits in a stepped-tandem arrangement for the WSO (forward) and the pilot (aft). The cockpit section has an internal 'bathtub' made of 10-mm (0$\frac{25}{64}$ in) aluminium alloy sheet to which 16-mm (0$\frac{5}{8}$ in) ceramic armour tiles are bonded. The glazing consists of optically flat bulletproof panels made of silicate glass; the windscreens and the side windows are 42 mm (1$\frac{21}{32}$ in) and 22 mm (0$\frac{55}{64}$ in) thick respectively. The cockpits are separated by an armoured bulkhead and have rearward-opening car-type doors (to port for the WSO and to starboard for the pilot). The doors, and the windows on the opposite side, can be jettisoned in an emergency. The forward fuselage incorporates a mount for the surveillance/targeting system pack (in a chin position) and a mount for the cannon turret (below the WSO's cockpit). The space below the pilot's cockpit houses an electrical equipment/avionics bay.

The *centre fuselage* tapering towards the rear is the primary structural assembly of the airframe. Its ceiling panel carries the main gearbox, the cooling fan, the hydraulic module, the APU and air conditioning system components. The centre fuselage mainframes have outrigger sections carrying the engines and incorporating attachment points for the stub wings. The lower part of the centre fuselage houses fuel tanks, with equipment items above them; the rear part of the equipment bay is normally unoccupied, serving as a cargo bay during redeployment. The fuselage sides feature numerous maintenance access hatches. The oval-section *tailboom* terminates in a moderately swept *tail rotor pylon* of airfoil section, the trailing-edge portion acting as a fixed rudder; an all-movable strut-braced stabiliser is mounted at the top of the pylon on the port side.

The nose of a Mi-28N tipped with a thimble radome for the ATGM guidance antenna, with the two optoelectronic 'turrets' of the surveillance/targeting system below it. The lower turret is reversed when not in use to protect the sensor window.

The cantilever mid-set anhedral stub wings have constant chord and no leading-edge sweep. They are all-metal, two-spar stressed-skin structures attached to the fuselage by explosive bolts allowing them to be jettisoned in an emergency. Each wing features two external stores pylons; the wingtips may be fitted with IRCM/ESM pods increasing overall span from 4.88 m (16 ft 0$\frac{1}{8}$ in) to 5.88 m (19 ft 3$\frac{1}{2}$ in).

The fixed tailwheel landing gear comprises levered-suspension main units with single wheels and pneumatic brakes and a castoring levered-suspension tail unit with a single non-braking wheel near the extremity of the tailboom. Steering on the ground is by differential braking. The main units have oleo-pneumatic shock absorbers with additional emergency travel in the event of a hard landing and allow the helicopter's ground clearance to be reduced for transportation by air.

The powerplant comprises two Izotov TV3-117VMA turboshafts with a 2,200-shp take-off rating and a 2,400-shp contingency rating, or two Klimov VK-2500-02 turboshafts with a 2,400-shp maximum take-off rating and a 2,700-shp contingency rating. Starting is by means of an air starter using compressed air from an Ivchenko AI-9V APU installed aft of the main gearbox. The engine nacelles taper off into an airfoil-like shape; the cowlings incorporate armour plating. The air intakes are fitted with vortex-type dust filters. Integral exhaust/air mixers are fitted, with intakes on the outboard side, and the engine exhausts are angled downwards.

Engine torque is fed via UR-28 bevel gearboxes into the VR-29 main gearbox which conveys torque to the main rotor, the accessories gearbox and the oil cooler fan; the latter is located aft of the main gearbox and has dorsal air intakes. A drive shaft on top of the tailboom connects the accessories gearbox to an intermediate gearbox at the base of the tail rotor pylon; thence a short shaft runs to the final drive gearbox. A rotor brake is provided.

The five-blade *main rotor* of 17.2 m (56 ft 5 in) diameter turns clockwise when seen from above. The rotor head is made of titanium and has spherical elastomeric hinges and metal/Teflon bearings. The constant-chord blades have raked tips and are of all-composite construction with a glassfibre spar and pockets with a glassfibre honeycomb structure. The four-blade pusher-type *tail rotor* of 3.85 m (12 ft 7$\frac{37}{64}$ in) diameter is

The cockpit section, showing the tinted bulletproof windows and the pilot's entry door, with a fairing below it housing an inflatable bag which is deployed for bailing out to stop the pilot from striking the undercarriage. The WSO's starboard window can be jettisoned in an emergency.

installed on the starboard side and turns anti-clockwise when seen from the hub; it consists of two pairs of blades superimposed in a squashed-X layout. The constant-chord blades are of similar all-composite design.

The fuel system features two independent subsystems feeding the port and starboard engines, with automatic cross-feed and pumping. It comprises three tanks (two service tanks and one common tank) placed in a container whose walls are lined with foam rubber for self-sealing; the fuel tanks are filled with explosion-suppression polyurethane foam. The fuel load is 1,500 kg (3,310 lb). All four wing pylons are plumbed for carrying drop tanks.

The Mi-24 has conventional mechanical flight controls, mostly with push-pull rods. Tail rotor pitch and stabiliser incidence are controlled by cables; the stabiliser control linkage is connected to the collective pitch lever. The control system features four hydraulic actuators placed on the main gearbox which act both as control actuators and as autopilot servos.

The hydraulic system comprises two independent subsystems which cater for the control actuators/servos and a hydraulic damper in the directional control circuit; the hydraulic pumps are driven off the accessory gearbox. The cockpit windshields, main and tail rotor blades and pitot heads are electrically de-iced. The air conditioning system uses bleed air from the engines or the APU. Also, the helicopter's equipment includes a pneumatic system and oxygen equipment.

The Mi-28 has an integrated avionics suite enabling the helicopter to fly and fight round the clock and in all weather conditions. The PrPNK-28 flight/navigation/attack suite developed by RPKB comprised the following components: a joint data processing system built around a Baghet-53 computer; a cockpit data presentation/input system with MFI-10-6M liquid-crystal

The 2A42 cannon and its NPPU-28 barbette.

The starboard wing with an eight-pack of 9M120 ATGMs on the outer pylon and a B-8V20 FFAR pod on the inboard pylon. The wingtip pod houses UV-26 flare dispensers (closed by covers in this case) and the sensors of the Otklik (Response) laser warning system.

The WSO's instrument panel with two MFI-10-6M multi-function displays and a PS-7V keypad/display. The electromechanical instruments are for back-up only.

multi-function displays and a PS-7V keypad; a navigation suite comprising the INS-2000 inertial navigation system, the SBKV-2V-2 platform-less attitude & heading reference system (linked to a satellite navigation channel, a Doppler speed/drift indicator and the air data system) and a long-range radio navigation (LORAN) system; an integrated radar warning & homing system/missile warning system with laser and UV detectors; an automatic flight control system; a weapons control system; a helmet-mounted cueing system (HMCS); a stabilised optoelectronic surveillance/targeting system with LLLTV/IR channels, a laser rangefinder and an auto-tracking feature; the pilot's observation/flight system with NVG; the helicopter's flight suite; and the KSS-28N-1 communications suite. The latter enables automatic secure data exchange with appropriately equipped ground command posts and other aircraft, using three channels. The avionics also include an ATT video image processor ensuring a clear image of the target in any lighting conditions. ESM/ECM/IRCM equipment includes the L-150-28 RHAWS, four UV-26 flare dispensers in wingtip pods and an active jammer; future Mi-28Ns will be equipped with the L370 Vitebsk ECM suite.

The Mi-28N is armed with a 30-mm 2A42 selectable-feed cannon on an NPPU-28 non-detachable mount installed under the nose, with an ammunition supply of 250 rounds in two cases (armour-piercing and HE/fragmentation/incendiary rounds). The cannon can be traversed through ±110° and elevated through +13 to –40°; it is aimed using the undernose surveillance/targeting system turret or the HMCS. Up to sixteen 9M120 Ataka-V or 9M114 Shtoorm-V supersonic ATGMs can be carried on racks fitted to the stub wing pylons; other air-to-surface weapons carried on the inboard pylons include two or four B-8V20 or B-13L1 FFAR pods with unguided rockets, S-24B heavy unguided rockets, GUV weapons pods, UPK-23-250 gun pods, KMGU-2 submunitions dispensers and 250- and 500-kg (551- and 1,102-lb) bombs or napalm containers. 9M39 Igla-V IR-homing AAMs can be carried in pairs for self-defence.

The crew rescue/protection system allows the crew to bail out safely in the event of an emergency occurring at altitudes above 100 m (330 ft). In this case the main rotor blades, stub wings and cockpit doors are jettisoned and the seat harness is cut automatically; inflatable bags are deployed below the doors to stop the crewmen from striking the landing gear. If the emergency occurs below 100 m and parachutes cannot be used, the Pamir-K energy-absorbing seats and other crashworthy features reduce the G loads inherent in a crash landing from 50-60 Gs to an acceptable 15-17 Gs.

Mi-28 BASIC DATA

	Mi-28	Mi-28A	Mi-28N
Powerplant type	2 x TV3-117VM	2 x TV3-117VMA	2 x VK-2500-02
Take-off power, shp	2 x 1,950	2 x 2,200	2 x 2,400
Empty weight, kg (lb)	7,900 (17,420)	8,095 (17,850)	8,590 (18,9401)
Weights, kg (lb):			
normal take-off weight	10,200 (22,490)	10,400 (22,930)	10,700 (23,590)
maximum take-off weight	11,200 (24,700)	11,500 (25,360)	12,000 (26,460)
Warload, kg (lb)	2,300 (5,070)	2,300 (5,070)	2,300 (5,070)
Speed, km/h (mph):			
maximum	300 (186)	300 (186)	324 (202)
cruising	270 (167)	265 (165)	265 (165)
Hovering ceiling OGE, m (ft)	3,470 (11,381)	3,600 (11,808)	3,700 (12,136)
Service ceiling, m (ft)	5,700 (18,696)	5,800 (19,024)	5,700 (18,696)
Operational range, km (miles)	435 (270)	460 (292)	460 (292)
Ferry range, km (miles)	1,100 (690)	1,100 (690)	1,100 (690)

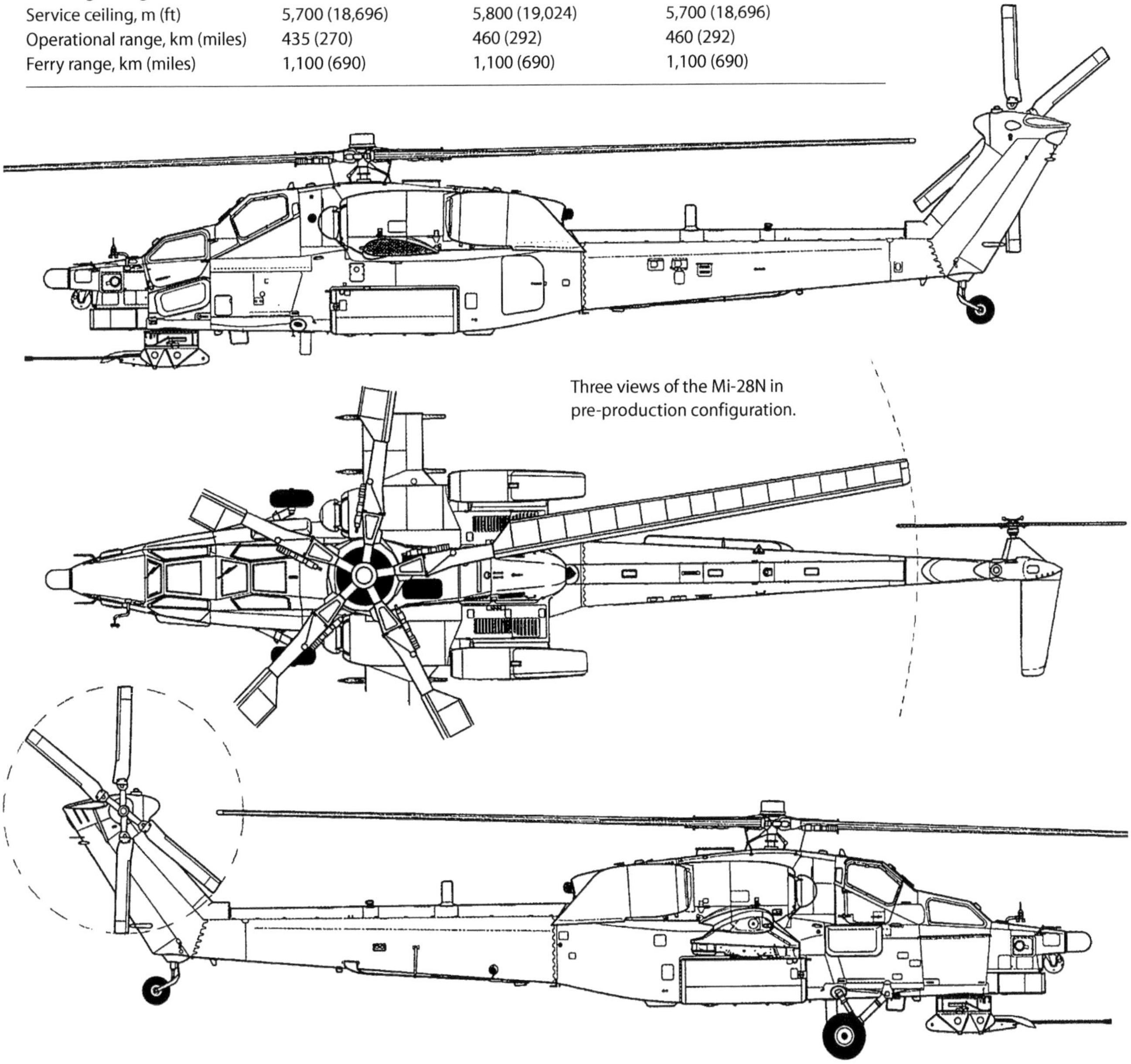

Three views of the Mi-28N in pre-production configuration.

The Modeller's Corner

MIL' **Mi-28** 1:72nd scale

So far there have been three injection moulded kits of the Mi-28 on the market, all to 1:72nd scale. The first one was issued by **Dragon Models** (aka **DML**, Ref. No. 2501); it was later reboxed by **Italeri** (Ref. No. 110) and later still by the Russian manufacturer **Zvezda** (**Mi-28A** *Havoc*, Ref. No. 7246). The kit features movable rotors and a movable cannon. The model does have a number of inaccuracies – the fuselage is a bit too narrow, the nose shape is wrong, the WSO's windshield has ended up rather too small and the WSO's cockpit door is not reproduced. The rotors, especially the main rotor hub, are rather crude; therefore some modellers recommend buying Zvezda's new Mi-35M kit and cannibalising it for the sake of the rotors.

Later, Zvezda issued a kit of the **Mi-28N** *Night Havoc* (*sic*, Ref. No. 7255). In so doing they made a replacement mould for the nose section, correcting the shape. However, rather than redo the entire fuselage they chose to include an extra sprue with the replacement nose (you have to cut off the old nose with a razor saw and mate the new one to the rest of the fuselage), and here's where the problem lies – the new accurate nose does not fit well!

Right and below:
Italeri's Mi-28A built 'out of the box' by Borislav Delov.

Bottom left to right:

The box top of Dragon's 1:72nd scale Mi-28A kit produced under licence by Italeri; note that the box carries the logos of both companies.

Close-up of the cannon installation. The sensor turret and the landing lights have been 'doctored' a bit by the modeller.

Close-up of the nose showing the utterly unrealistic proportions of the front cockpit glazing.

Three views of Zvezda's Mi-28N built 'out of the box' by 'kent'.

Below left: Close-up of the Mi-28N model's new nose section.

Below: The box top of Zvezda's 1:72nd scale Mi-28N kit.

Right: Another Zvezda Mi-28N in the process of assembly by a different modeller.

The second **Mi-28A** kit is by **Revell** (Ref. No. 4489). The kit comprises 70 parts and the finished model has movable rotors and a movable cannon. Again, Revell subsequently reissued the kit with extra parts as the **Mi-28N**. Overall, the Revell kit captures the looks of the *Havoc* much better, but the impression is spoiled by the main rotor which sits unnaturally high above the fuselage on a tall mast.

The third **Mi-28A** kit was manufactured by a South Korean company called **Lee** (Ref. No. 00106). There have been claims that the Mi-28 kit that was marketed in Russia by the St. Petersburg-based **Modelist** (Ref. No. 207224) is actually a rebox of Lee's. Yet there have also been claims that Lee is identical to Zvezda. A rebox of a rebox?

Finally, there is evidence of a Mi-28 kit marketed under the **Testors** brand. The box art shows a photo of the finished mode that can only be described as Ye Awfulle Modelle, since it faithfully reproduces the wildly inaccurate artist's impression of the Mi-28 that appeared in the western press back in the mid-1980s.

The only aftermarket item available for the 1:72nd scale Mi-28 is a set of correct Pamir-K crew seats cast in resin by **Heliborne**.

Far right: The box top of Testors' 1:72nd scale Mi-28A kit shows a horrid parody of the *Havoc* – the model is based on early artist's impressions found in the western press in the 1980s.

Left and below: The same model following completion.

Centre left: The box top of Revell's 1:72nd scale Mi-28N kit.

Centre right and bottom: The Revell Mi-28N built 'out of the box' by Dan Duna. The model was painted with Testors acrylic paints.

'032 Yellow', the third prototype Mi-28 representing the Mi-28A day-only version.

'35 Yellow', the fourth pre-production Mi-28N operated by the 344th Combat Training & Aircrew conversion Centre at Torzhok.

Mi-28N '05 Blue', 387th Aviation Base, Budyonnovsk. The helicopter crashed on 15th February 2011.

Mi-28N '02 Red'/'RF-95648, still in camouflage colours but with Russian star insignia and 'VVS Rossii' (Russian Air Force) titles.

Mi-28N '08 Red'/RF-95654 has a bolder camouflage scheme and differently positioned Russian Air Force titles.

'47 Yellow'/RF-, another Mi-28N from Torzhok, in current overall grey colours.

Kamov Ka-52

The Alligator

By the early 1980s the USA and the other NATO nations had built up a large fleet of specialised attack helicopters tailored for CAS and combating armoured vehicles. The Soviet Mi-24 was not quite in the same league, being larger and heavier and having a secondary assault transport role (unlike the western attack choppers). When Hughes Aircraft brought out the AH-64A Apache, the Mil' OKB responded by developing the Mi-28 along similar lines. This was the helicopter the Soviet MoD placed its bets on; when a competitor appeared on the scene, initially it enjoyed scant support.

The competitor was OKB-938 – the design bureau named after Nikolay I. Kamov, which until then had specialised in naval (shipboard) and civil utility helicopters utilising the co-axial layout. True to form, the Kamov OKB used the same layout for their army attack helicopter project which bore the designation V-80 or *izdeliye* 800. Its uniqueness among attack helicopters lay not only in the layout; unlike all other combat helicopters, the V-80 was a single-seater. Kamov OKB engineers believed that automation of many functions would allow a single pilot to cope with the mission. A suite of four digital computers would be responsible for navigation, weapons application, operation of the ECM/ESM/IRCM suite and health & usage monitoring of the helicopter's systems.

The V-80 had a slender fuselage, the cockpit having optically flat bulletproof glazing and a portside car-type door. The tail unit consisted of a virtually all-movable fin and stabilisers with endplate fins mounted further forward. Like other helicopters in the class, the V-80 had stub wings with external stores pylons and ESM/IRCM pods at the tips. The tricycle landing gear was retractable. The TV3-117VM engines were identical to the Mi-28's and likewise installed laterally. The armament was the same as on the Mi-28 but the 2A42 cannon was mounted on the starboard side of the fuselage, with very limited traversing/elevation angles, which meant the pilot had to aim it by pointing the whole chopper; on the other hand, the co-axial layout facilitated this, making the helicopter less sensitive to crosswinds. The missile armament consisting of 9M4172 Vikhr' (Whirlwind; AT-16 *Scallion*) ATGMs was new; the long-range missiles were to be guided automatically, theoretically enabling the V-80 to engage enemy tanks while staying out of range of the enemy's AA weapons. The extreme nose housed the *Mer**koo**riy* (Mercury, the planet) targeting/guidance system.

One more unique feature of the V-80 was its crew rescue system. In the event of a catastrophic failure or shootdown the rotor blades were jettisoned, whereupon the pilot was ejected upwards. The K-37-800 ejection seat was specially developed for the V-80 by the Zvezda (Star) Research & Production Enterprise and featured a squib extracting the seat.

The first prototype made its maiden flight on 17th June 1982, followed by four others in 1983, 1985, 1989 and 1990. Design issues were not the only problem the Kamov OKB had to deal with when developing the V-80; the unconventional helicopter was facing stiff opposition, including a good many generals who held high posts in the Soviet MoD. Critics slammed both the single-seat concept (because of the high pilot workload associated with flying and aiming the weapons at once in an air defence environment) and the co-axial layout which they cited as unsuitable for a battlefield chopper due to the danger of blade collision during sharp manoeuvres (here they had a point, as later events showed). A flyoff between the V-80 and the Mi-28 in September-October 1986 showed that the latter type was superior. Yet the Kamov lobby in the MoD was strong enough to secure a decision ordering the helicopter into production as the Ka-50; low-rate production at AAPO Progress in Arsen'yev commenced in 1991 under the product code *izdeliye* 805. The Ka-50 received the popular name ***Chor**naya **a**koo**la*** (Black Shark) and the NATO reporting name *Hokum*. The helicopter also had experimental night-capable versions – the Ka-50Sh and Ka-50N.

The trials, which were held in conditions replicating a battle scenario as closely as possible, showed that the Ka-50 did have its weaknesses. Obviously the adversary would seek to extend the 'kill' range and reduce the reaction time of its air defence systems, and the Ka-50 was by no means invulnerable. To reduce combat losses among attack helicopters, the US Army and the Israeli Defence Force/Air Force resorted to using special battlefield surveillance helicopters equipped with a mast-mounted sight. For example, AH-64A attack helicopters operated jointly with Bell OH-58D Kiowa Warrior combat scout helicopters; as a successor to the OH-58D, Boeing and Sikorsky jointly developed the LHX (later known as the RAH-66

25

Comanche), but this programme eventually fell victim to defence budget cuts. In the Soviet Union/Russia, the Mi-24K was optimised for target designation in the interests of artillery and multiple launcher rocket system units, not helicopter units. Knowing this, the Kamov OKB started work on the V-60 compact and agile combat scout helicopter, but *perestroika* and the ensuing turmoil prevented the project from coming to fruition.

The operation of the Ka-50's automated avionics suite that was to permit single-pilot operations was far from perfect, and the debugging effort dragged on and on. The Russian MoD refused to accept the brand-new Ka-50s built by AAPO Progress and pay for them, putting the plant on the verge of bankruptcy.

Acknowledging that some of the military's complaints regarding the Ka-50 were justified and being aware that developing a 'clean sheet of paper' combat helicopter was out of the question, now that Russia was in the throes of a political and financial crisis, General Designer Sergey V. Mikheyev proposed developing a two-seat version of the *Hokum*. This would be a combat scout helicopter, the second crewman being a mission equipment operator; when the helicopter popped up over the battlefield he would assess the situation and designate targets for helicopters in a group, acting as commander.

Development of the two-seater, which was designated **Ka-52**, proceeded under the *Avangard-1* (Vanguard-1) R&D programme. A rather provisional mock-up was presented to the State commission in 1994 together

Opposite page:
'25 Yellow', a typical production Ka-50. The black portions of the tail unit and the starboard forward fuselage side are 'anti-soot' paint.

Here, '25 Yellow' shows off its undersides during a flying display. Note the tandem antennas of the Doppler speed/drift sensor under the tailboom, the mounts for additional optoelectronic systems ahead of the mainwheels and the missile warning sensors flanking the forward fuselage and tailboom.

This page:
This photo of two *Hokum-As* flying over the Russian countryside shows why the Ka-50 has been dubbed Black Shark. Note that '24 Yellow' is fitted with exhaust/air mixers while '26 Yellow' is not; there are other detail differences as well.

With the landing gear in mid-retraction, Ka-50 '27 Yellow' shows details of its port side. 500-litre drop tanks are suspended on the inboard pylons.

with the project documents. When the first information on the project was circulated in the media, some experts wasted no time declaring that 'the single-seat combat helicopter concept had flopped'. In reality, however, the Ka-52 was meant to complement the Ka-50, not replace it – just like the RAH-66 would have complemented the AH-64, had it been fielded. The Ka-52 was not a rejection but a development of the original Ka-50 concept to suit the changing scenario of a limited war or anti-terrorist operation – one which Russia would face that same year.

The usual tandem seating arrangement was unsuitable for the Ka-52 because it entailed a long armour capsule and hence more weight away from the CG, which would impair manoeuvrability. Therefore the crewmen were seated side by side in a wider cockpit on K-37-800M seats. Another factor in favour of this was that side-by-side seating facilitated crew communication – even a gesture could be enough to convey the message, saving vital time in combat. Importantly, cross-section area was almost unchanged, as the Ka-50's fuselage was widest aft of the cockpit. The Ka-52's flattened snout with windshield halves resembling 'eyes' gave rise to a new popular name – Alligator.

The designers strove to retain maximum structural and systems commonality with the Ka-50 – even down to flat windshields and car-type doors. Later the cockpit was revised to cut drag and improve ergonomics, featuring a more streamlined windshield and upward-opening canopy doors, as well as liquid-crystal MFDs instead of electromechanical instruments and a cathode-ray tube display. Commonality was thus reduced from 95% to 85%, but most of the shortcomings pointed out by the State commission were rectified.

The main difference from the Ka-50 lay in the mission avionics. The Ka-52 was equipped with a *Sam**shit*** (Boxwood) optoelectronic surveillance/targeting system featuring TV/LLLTV, IR and laser ranging channels and having an auto-tracking feature. In daytime clear-weather conditions it could detect and identify a tank at 15 km (9.3 miles) range. An RN01 Arbalet-52 millimetre-waveband radar developed by Phazotron-NIIR was fitted; it was capable of detecting a tank at 20 km (12.4 miles) range and had a mapping mode.

The prototype was converted from the second production Ka-50 in 1996. When it was rolled out on 12th November that year, the Ka-52 (then known as *izdeliye* 806) had the large 'ball turret' of the Samshit system mounted dorsally aft of the cockpit; the radar's main antenna occupied the parabolic nose radome, and there was also a secondary antenna in a small pill-shaped radome on top of the radar mast for detecting aerial targets – even incoming missiles. The beginning of flight tests was delayed by the decision to demonstrate the helicopter at the Aero India-96 airshow in Bangalore; after that, the Ka-52 received the reporting name *Hokum-B*, the Ka-50 becoming the *Hokum-A*. The Alligator finally made its first flight on 25th June 1997 at the hands of Aleksandr Smirnov and Dmitriy Titov.

Being heavier than the Ka-50, the Ka-52 held an uncomfortable first place among coaxial-rotor helicopters as regards rotor disc loading, which impaired its flight performance as compared to the precursor. Luckily the VR-80 gearbox was designed with sufficient strength reserves to permit installation of more powerful engines. Accordingly the Russian NPP Klimov engine design bureau and the Ukrainian Motor Sich engine factory teamed up to create a new version of the engine designated TV3-117VMA-F (*for**seer**ovannyy* – uprated); its take-off power was increased from 2,225 to 2,500 shp, with a contingency rating of 2,800 shp. The engine had a new electrohydraulic control system giving better acceleration and higher surge resistance during rocket launches, and there was an automatic relight function in the event of flameout. An alternative engine, the VK-2500 (alias TV3-117VMA-SB3), offered slightly less power (2,400 shp and 2,700 shp respectively) but had a lower fuel consumption and more than twice the designated service life (7,500 hours versus 3,000 hours).

A whole bunch of problems was associated with the surveillance/targeting suite. Quite apart from the fact that the dorsal position of the Samshit system did not afford it a sufficient downward field of view, the system itself had failed to meet its specifications (the 'some s**t' sound of the name turned out to be true, after all). First, two secondary optoelectronic 'ball turrets' were added under the nose but apparently this was not good enough. Next, the nose radome was cut away to accommodate a drum-shaped turret with a Rotor optoelectronic system, but this left no room for the radar antenna; the mast-mounted secondary antenna was not working properly, and eliminating the radar altogether would severely limit the Ka-52's all-weather capability.

Defining and debugging the Ka-52's mission avionics took several years. The end result was the *Argu**ment**-2000* flight/navigation/attack suite which included the GOES-451 optoelectronic surveillance/targeting system and the Arbalet-52 radar. The GOES-451 can work round the clock and in fog; its large 'ball turret' is located ventrally immediately ahead of the nose gear unit, not encroaching on the radome. The flight/navigation/attack suite, ECM/ESM/IRCM suite and the BKS-50 communications suite are integrated via the Baghet-53 computer. The latter allows new systems to be integrated easily by updating the software.

The 9A4172 Vikhr' ATGM inherited from the Ka-50 was regarded as the Ka-52's principal weapon. The missile has automated laser guidance and a tandem shaped-charge armour-piercing/HE/fragmentation warhead capable of penetrating armour equiva-

The first prototype Ka-52, '061 White outline', in an early configuration with the dorsal Samshit 'ball turret', two small ventral optoelectronic turrets and mast-mounted radome.

lent to 900-mm (35 7/16 in) homogeneous steel armour at 8 km (5 miles) range; explosive reactive armour (ERA) is no problem for it. The missile is superior to the US AGM-114A Hellfire. Later the Tula Instrument Design Bureau responsible for the missile brought out the Vikhr'-M version with 9M4172 missiles in various versions. At a range of 400 m to 10 km (0.25-6.2 miles) the Ka-52 armed with Vikhr'-M missiles can score a 'kill' against a tank with 1,000-mm (39⅜ in) armour and ERA with 80% probability and engage four different targets within 30 seconds.

Yet, the Vikhr' missile system turned out to be extremely complex and expensive, while its debugging was hampered by chronic funding shortages and general turmoil in the 1990s. Therefore, as an alternative the Ka-52 can use the less sophisticated but relatively cheap and trouble-free 9M120 Ataka (AT-9 *Spiral*) ATGM in its laser-guided version; the missile can destroy a tank with 800-mm (31½ in) armour and ERA with at least 65% probability. Improved versions – the 9M120M capable of penetrating 950-mm (37 13/32 in) armour, the 9M120F with a HE warhead for use against fortifications and the 9M220 AAM – were also developed. On the other hand, the Ataka missiles are no good against current NATO air defence systems which can destroy the helicopter at up to 4 km (2.5 miles) range in 4-10 seconds with 100% probability before the chopper has a chance to neutralise them; only the Vikhr' missile system allows the Ka-52 to attack from beyond the range of Roland, Stinger, Mistral and Guepard AA systems. Additionally, the *Hokum-B* is able to use Kh-25ML (AS-10 *Karen*) laser-guided air-to-surface missiles normally carried by fixed-wing strike aircraft.

Here, '061 White outline' in the same configuration is seen parked at Zhukovskiy.

Right: A later configuration of the same machine with the Rotor optoelectronic system in a drum-shaped turret in the nose and no radar.

Other weapons used by the Ka-52 include 20-tube B-8V20 pods with 80-mm S-8 FFARs (available in 15 versions with different warheads), B-13L1 pods with five 122-mm S-13 FFARs each, S-24 heavy unguided rockets, and free-fall bombs. The latter are traditionally part of the Soviet/Russian combat helicopters' arsenal and are often the most cost-effective solution. By comparison, the AH-64 does not carry bombs and uses FFARs of smaller calibre (68 mm).

The 2A42 cannon was likewise inherited from the Ka-50. Western experts have often criticised this weapon for its weight – the 2A42, complete with the NPPU-80 mount, weighs 115 kg (253.5 lb) versus 54.4 kg (120 lb) for the Hughes M230 30-mm cannon fitted to the AH-64. However, the Soviet cannon has much greater range –4 km (2.5 miles) versus 1.5 km (0.93 miles) – and uses more lethal rounds; at 1.5 km range they penetrate 15-mm ($0\frac{19}{32}$ in) steel armour when impacting at 60°. Also, the 2A42 uses the same ammunition as Soviet/Russian IFVs, which facilitates logistics when a mechanised or airborne forces group is supported by choppers; in contrast, the M230 requires aviation ammunition (M789 and M799 rounds, with ammo for the British ADEN and French DEFA cannons as a substitute). The Ka-52's ammunition supply is 470 rounds; the AH-64 has a maximum of 1,200 rounds but normally carries only 320.

As mentioned earlier, the cannon is mounted on the starboard side and is, to all intents and purposes, fixed – the Ka-52 pilot must point the whole chopper at the target in order to fire. However, this disadvantage is offset by the co-axial layout (which is less sensitive to crosswinds, allowing the Ka-52 to fly sideways at high speed) and the placement of the cannon close to the CG, which minimises the effect of the recoil. Also, pilots find it easier to look ahead, not sideways, when taking aim. In addition to the built-in cannon, two UPK-23-250 cannon pods may be carried – a potent weapon against lightly armoured vehicles and AA assets at close range.

For self-defence against enemy aircraft the Ka-52 may carry four 9M39 Igla-V IR-homing AAMs – an air-launched version of the Igla MANPADS. The pilot is provided with an ILS-28K head-up display which may be used for attacking both ground and aerial targets.

The Kamov Company cites several advantages of the Ka-52's co-axial layout, including higher efficiency (no engine power is lost for driving the anti-torque tail rotor); this gives the advantage of 6-10% better acceleration from the hover as compared to conventional helicopters when attacking from an ambush. Inertia forces are lower because on a compact co-axial layout helicopter the heavy items are closer to the CG. In a helicopter duel the Ka-52 pilot finds it easier to bring his weapons to bear on the target by making a flat pedal turn; a conventional helicopter requires more time to get into position for an attack. When attacking a ground target the Ka-52 can execute the 'funnel' manoeuvre, orbiting the target while keeping the nose pointing at it all the while. It can also manoeuvre vigorously over hilly terrain, dodging the obstacles or 'jumping' over them, which makes it easier to neutralise enemy AA installations (giving them less time to react) – even at night, using a special mode of the radar.

While the co-axial layout may be seen as a liability from a survivability standpoint (there are more rotor blades to hit), it also helps survivability, as directional control is retained even if the rudder is shot away. Speaking of which, the rotor blade spars are designed to survive hits by 12.7-mm heavy machine-gun bullets and 20-mm shell fragments. Armour plating is provided to protect the crew and vital items against 12.7-mm HMG fire and high-energy missile/AA shell fragments. Vital piping, wiring and control runs are duplicated for reliability. Exhaust/

Opposite page: Here, '061 White outline' is seen at a still later date with an optoelectronic 'ball turret' underneath a 'shark snout'. The helicopter carries 9A4172 Vikhr' ATGMs.

The first prototype in a new two-tone camouflage as '061 Yellow'. The nose has reverted to its original shape and there are no optoelectronic 'turrets' whatever. The pod under the port wing is apparently associated with test equipment.

air mixers can be fitted to reduce the IR signature and protect against heat-seeking missiles. As noted earlier, the Ka-52 has a crew ejection system. Unlike the Ka-50, where the cockpit roof is jettisoned before the seat fires, on the two-seater ejection takes place through the canopy, which – for the first time on a Russian helicopter – incorporates micro detonating cords. In the event of a crash landing the undercarriage and the crashworthy seats will help cushion the impact, preventing crew injury.

An important advantage of the Ka-52 is that the side-by-side layout obviates the

need for a specialised trainer version. The helicopter has dual controls and one of the pilots can act as instructor, monitoring the trainee's actions.

AAPO Progress had started gearing up for Ka-52 production back in 1997, but the programme suffered delays due to lack of funding and other reasons. Not until 2008 did the plant manufacture the second and third prototypes; the former of these took to the air on 27th June. By then the helicopter's product code had changed to *izdeliye* 826 – apparently to reflect the design changes that had been made. The second and third prototypes had the ventral GOES-451 'turret' and provisions for two small optoelectronic system 'turrets' near the main gear units, but as yet no radar. They took part in the State acceptance trials; Stage A of these was completed in late 2008 and the go-ahead was given to build an initial production batch that would be used for Stage B.

Production picked up pace slowly. In 2009 the 344th Combat Training & Aircrew Conversion Centre in Torzhok took delivery of three pre-production Ka-52s – the only ones completed that year; these and subsequent *Hokum-Bs* differed in having enhanced armour protection for the crew. At the end of the year the Russian MoD placed an initial order for 36 Ka-52s. In 2010 the Russian Air Force began receiving production Ka-52s powered by VK-2500 engines. The first four of these likewise went to Torzhok.

The State acceptance trials of the Ka-52 – now fully equipped – were completed in 2011. On 19th May that year it was the turn of the first operational unit – the 575th Army Aviation Base (formerly 319th Independent Helicopter Regiment) at Chernigovka in the Russian Far East – to get its first four *Hokum-B*; three more followed in short order, and the unit was expected to re-equip completely from the Mi-24 before long. That year AAPO Progress delivered nine Ka-52s, the last four of which were fully equipped; the missing radar would be retrofitted to the ones already built in due course. In August 2011 the Russian MoD's acquisition agency Oboronprom and the Russian Helicopters holding company (of which Kamov is part) signed a long-term contract for the delivery of 140 Ka-52s to the Russian Armed Forces.

As noted earlier, the Ka-52 is now regarded as a helicopter for the Special Forces; it will be used in anti-terrorist operations – notably in the North Caucasus where guerrilla gangs with al-Qaeda affiliations are active even as of this writing. Its fielding comes as a major boost, enabling joint-service operations in any weather round the clock, especially if the targets are carefully concealed; automated data exchange with ground command posts and other aircraft will make sure that upcoming threats are neutralised quicker.

Attempts were also made to market the Ka-52 internationally. First, in late 1997 Kamov joined the Turkish Air Force's new attack helicopter contest, offering the **Ka-50-2 Erdoğan** ('warrior' in Turkish) – a two-seat derivative of the Ka-50 with tandem cockpits to meet the customer's requirement. After much wrangling the project got no further than a full-size mock-up.

The second try was when the *Hokum-B* was entered into the South Korean Air Force's new attack helicopter contest announced on 19th April 2000, competing against the Bell AH-1Z Viper, Boeing AH-64D Apache Longbow, Sikorsky AUH-60 Black Hawk, Eurocopter EC 665 Tiger, Agusta A129INT Mangusta – and the Mi-28NE. The version for the Korean tender was known as the **Ka-52K** (the first thus designated); the K denoted either *k**o**reyskiy* (Korean) or *k**ommer**cheskiy* ('commercial', i.e., export). The export version was to feature French, Belgian and Israeli avionics as specified by the customer. The Koreans were given a tour of the AAPO Progress plant, and the Korean pilots were given a ride in the Ka-52 that included live firing, but no order ensued. China also sized up the Ka-52, but the Chinese wanted to buy a manufacturing licence, not ready-made helicopters.

In 2011 the Ka-52 unexpectedly 'returned to its naval origins'. A year earlier Russia had ordered two *Mistral* class amphibious assault ships from France for delivery in 2014-15 and bought a licence to build two more – a highly controversial deal in more than one aspect. Thankfully at least the helicopters making up the ships' carrier wing are indigenous; the first two Russian Navy Mistrals (provisionally christened RNS *Vladivostok* and RNS *Sevastopol'*) are to be equipped with Ka-27 *Helix-A* anti-submarine warfare helicopters, Ka-29 *Helix-B* transport/assault helicopters – and Ka-52s. The designation **Ka-52K** was reused for the navalised version, the K denoting *kora-**bel'**nyy* (shipboard) in this case; the helicopter differs from the baseline army model in having folding rotor blades (similar to those of the Ka-27/Ka-29) and folding stub wings for on-deck/below-deck stowage, a reinforced landing gear with tie-down shackles, and enhanced corrosion protection for operations in a maritime environment. The avionics will feature a special broadband communications suite that will be responsible both for data exchange with the ship and for navigation/carrier approach.

The shipboard version was first revealed by Anatoliy Isaykin, head of the Rosoboronexport arms export agency, at the 49th Paris Air Show on 20th June 2011; on 26th July that year the Kamov Company's General Designer Sergey V. Mikheyev announced plans to build the first batch of Ka-52Ks by 2014. Back in November 2009, when FNS *Mistral* had paid a visit to St.-Petersburg, a standard Ka-52 had made deck landings on the ship in an improvised carrier compatibility test; now in August-September 2011 the original Ka-52 prototype passed initial sea trials, making several

Above and left: '062 Yellow', the second prototype, wore green/tan camouflage that was initially standard for the type. Here it is seen carrying no fewer than four ventral optoelectronic system turrets, the largest of these housing a GOES-451 targeting system. The large pod under the port wing accommodates test equipment.

Left: '063 Yellow', the third prototype, was painted in two-tone grey camouflage. Here the main undernose optoelectronic system turret is missing. Note the ESM antenna 'eggs' on top of the wingtip pods and the 'six-pack' of 9M120 ATGMs.

51

51

Opposite page:
The first pre-production Ka-52, '51 Yellow', represents the production configuration of the *Hokum-B*, except that the secondary optoelectronic system turrets near the main gear units are not installed. Note the large radome for the Arbalet-52 radar and the additional armour plates on the canopy doors.

This page:
Pre-production Ka-52 '52 Yellow' shares the hardstand at Kubinka with a Mi-28N.

'53 Yellow', the third pre-production example, with drop tanks, 'six-pack' and test equipment pod. Note the GOES-451 painted in the same bluish grey colour as the undersurfaces (rather than black).

'92 Yellow', an initial production Ka-52 operated by the 344th Combat Training & Aircrew conversion Centre at Torzhok.

'98 Yellow', an example from the second batch of Ka-52s delivered to Torzhok, illustrates the current grey finish of production *Hokum-Bs*.

flights from the helipad of the North Fleet ASW cruiser RNS *Vice-Admiral Kulakov* with good results. On 7th August 2012 a Russian Helicopters spokesman stated that construction of the Ka-52K prototypes had begun. Until the amphibious assault ships are commissioned with the Pacific Fleet, with eight *Helix-A/Bs* and eight *Hokum-Bs* each, the first Ka-52Ks will operate from the Russian Navy's sole aircraft carrier RNS *Fleet Admiral Kuznetsov*. The naval version's reporting name is *Hokum-B Mod*.

In November 2012 the Russian MoD announced its intention to test the Ka-52 in actual combat against Somalian pirates. To this end a number of Ka-52s are to be redeployed to the French base in Djibouti (by sea or by air if the runway at Djibouti-Ambouli AB can handle Antonov An-124 Ruslan transports). According to a source in the Russian MoD, the decision to use the Alligator for these operations was prompted by the fact that the Ka-52K is to equip the carrier wing of the Russian Navy's future *Mistral* class amphibious assault ships; also, tropical seas are the best proving ground (oops) for shipboard helicopter forces.

THE Ka-52 IN DETAIL

The following brief description applies to the production Ka-52.

The fuselage is built in three sections and is made of aluminium alloy and composites. The *forward fuselage* incorporates the cockpit with side-by-side seating for the pilot (left) and the WSO (right). The cockpit is protected by steel and aluminium armour. It has a fixed windshield (with two optically flat bulletproof windscreen panels and curved sidelights) and two upward-opening glazed sections (with armour plate inserts) hinged to a centreline frame member; the windscreens are made of silicate glass and the rest of the glazing is Plexiglas. An avionics bay ahead of the cockpit houses the radar set and incorporates a ventral ring mount for the surveillance/targeting system turret; the radar antenna is enclosed by a large parabolic glassfibre radome opening to port. The space below the cockpit houses the nosewheel well.

The *centre fuselage* of rectangular cross-section with rounded corners is the primary structural assembly of the airframe. It accommodates the main gearbox, the cooling fan, the APU, the fuel tanks, the mainwheel wells, hydraulic system and air conditioning system components. The centre fuselage is flanked by the engine nacelles separated from the surrounding bays by firewalls. A vertically disposed ring mount for the cannon is located ahead of the starboard mainwheel well, with a recess for the cannon barrel ahead of it. The *rear fuselage* tapering towards the rear incorporates avionics/equipment bays with large lateral access panels and the stabiliser carry-through structure.

The cantilever mid-set *stub wings* have strong incidence and zero dihedral. They are an all-metal, two-spar stressed-skin structure built in three pieces – a centre section built integrally with the fuselage (terminating outboard of the engine nacelles) and two detachable panels with pronounced taper and no leading-edge sweep. Each outer wing features two external stores pylons; the wingtips carry elliptical IRCM/ESM pods with dorsal and ventral strakes at the rear.

The tail unit comprises a small moderately swept fin with a large sharply swept root fillet (built integrally with the rear fuselage), a large horn-balanced rudder with a fixed trim tab, and shoulder-mounted fixed-incidence cantilever stabilisers; the latter have upturned trailing-edge portions and hexagonal endplates. The fin and the stabiliser carry-through structure are of metal construction; the rudder and the detachable stabiliser panels-cum-endplates are made of carbonfibre reinforced plastic.

The hydraulically-retractable tricycle landing gear comprises a castoring levered-suspension nose unit with twin 400x150 mm (15.74x5.90 in) non-braking wheels and a shimmy damper and main units with single 700x250 mm (27.55x9.84 in) wheels and hydraulic brakes. Wheel track 2.67 m (8 ft 9 7/64 in), wheelbase 4.611 m (15 ft 1 17/32 in). Steering on the ground is by differential braking. All units retract aft; the nose unit is semi-exposed when retracted, the mainwheels stow vertically flush with the fuselage sides, the outer faces remaining exposed, while the oleos are closed by tandem doors opening only when the gear is in transit. All three units feature ground resonance dampers.

The powerplant comprises two Klimov VK-2500 turboshafts with a 2,400-shp maximum take-off rating and a 2,700-shp contingency rating. Starting is by means of an air starter using compressed air from an Ivchenko AI-9V APU installed transversely aft of the main gearbox, with the exhaust on the starboard side. The engine cowlings incorporate armour plating and double as maintenance platforms. The air intakes are fitted with vortex-type dust filters. The engine exhausts can be fitted with exhaust/air mixers angled outwards. The fire suppression system caters for the engines, APU, main gearbox and cooling fan; the first shot is discharged automatically.

Engine torque is fed via bevel gearboxes into the VR-80 main gearbox which conveys torque to the rotors, the accessories gearbox and the oil cooler fan. The rotor system comprises two co-axial three-blade rotors mounted on a tall rotor mast; the upper rotor turns clockwise and the lower one anticlockwise when seen from above. The rotors have hingeless torsion-bar hubs; the constant-chord blades have raked tips and are of composite construction.

The fuel system features two self-sealing bag-type tanks acting as service tanks (the front tank feeds the port engine, the rear one feeds the starboard engine and APU), with automatic cross-feed and pumping. The fuel tanks are filled with explosion-suppression polyurethane foam. The internal fuel load is 1,487 kg (3,278 lb). All four wing pylons are plumbed for carrying 500-litre (110 Imp. gal) drop tanks, the port ones being connected to the rear tank and the starboard ones to the front tank.

The Ka-52 has conventional mechanical flight controls with push-pull rods and hydraulic actuators. Full dual controls are provided, enabling either crewman to fly the helicopter. The control system has a feature increasing the cyclic and collective pitch lever forces as a warning if the danger of blade collision arises during manoeuvres.

The hydraulic system comprises two independent subsystems. The *main system* caters for the control actuators/servos and emergency gear extension; the *common system* caters for the landing gear, the cannon mount and serves as a back-up feed for the control actuators. The cockpit windshields, rotor blades and pitot heads are electrically de-iced; the engine air intakes and filters have hot-air de-icing. The electric system uses 115 V/400 Hz AC supplied by two 400-kW generators driven off the accessory gearbox. The air conditioning system uses bleed air from the engines or the APU. Besides, the helicopter's equipment includes a pneumatic system and oxygen equipment.

The Ka-52 has an Argument-2000 integrated avionics suite enabling the helicopter to fly and fight round the clock and in all weather conditions. The suite includes a joint data processing system built around a Baghet-53 computer; a cockpit data presentation/input system with liquid-crystal MFDs and a wide-angle HUD; a navigation suite; an automatic flight control system; a weapons control system; a helmet-mounted cueing system (HMCS); an RN01 Arbalet-52 radar; a GOES-451 stabilised optoelectronic surveillance/targeting system; and the BKS-50 communications suite (comprising three radios, a scrambler and data link equipment). ESM/ECM/IRCM equipment includes an L-370V52 defensive electronics suite is provided; it includes RHAWS and MWS sensors giving 360° coverage. Four UV-26 flare dispensers are installed in the wingtip pods.

Ka-52 BASIC DATA

Length, rotors turning	15.862 m (52 ft 0 3 1/64 in)
Fuselage length	13.87 m (45 ft 6 in)
Height on ground	5.01 m (16 ft 5 15/64 in)
Wing span	7.835 m (25 ft 8 15/32 in)
Rotor diameter	14.5 m (47 ft 6 55/64 in)
Rotor disc area, m^2 (sq. ft)	165.046 (1,774.68)
Empty weight, kg (lb)	7,800 (17,195)
Take-off weight, kg (lb):	
normal	10,400 (22,930)
maximum	10,800 (23,810)
ferry configuration	12,200 (26,900)
Payload, kg (lb)	2,500 (5,510)
Max speed, km/h (mph)	300 (186)
Cruising speed, km/h (mph)	260 (161)
Max rate of climb, m/sec	
(ft/min): at sea level	12.0 (2,350)
at 2,500 m (8,200 ft)	9.0 (1,770)
Hovering ceiling OGE, m (ft)	3,900 (12,800)
Service ceiling, m (ft)	5,500 (18,040)
Operational range, km (miles)	460 (285)
Ferry range, km (miles)	1,110 (689)

The cockpit of Ka-52 '063 Yellow', showing the six MFDs and the dual controls.

The Ka-52 is armed with a 30-mm 2A42 selectable-feed cannon on an NPPU-80 non-detachable mount on the starboard side of the centre fuselage, with an ammunition supply of 460 rounds in two cases (armour-piercing and HE/fragmentation/incendiary rounds). The cannon can be traversed through 2°30' left/9° right and elevated through +3°30' to –37°; it is aimed using the undernose surveillance/targeting system turret or the HMCS. Up to twelve 9M120 Ataka-V or 9M113V Shtoorm-VU supersonic ATGMs can be carried on 'six-pack' racks fitted to the outer wing pylons; other air-to-surface weapons carried on the wing pylons include two or four B-8V20 or B-13L1 FFAR pods, S-24B heavy unguided rockets, UPK-23-250 gun pods, KMGU-2 submunitions dispensers and 250- and 500-kg (551- and 1,102-lb) bombs. 9M39 Igla-V IR-homing AAMs can be carried in pairs for self-defence.

The crew rescue system comprises two Zvezda K-37-800M ejection seats permitting ejection from down to zero level. The rotor blades are jettisoned and the canopy glazing is shattered by micro detonating cords before ejection.

The cockpit of a production Ka-52. The electromechanical back-up instruments and one of the smaller MFDs have been repositioned, apparently in response to the pilots' comments.

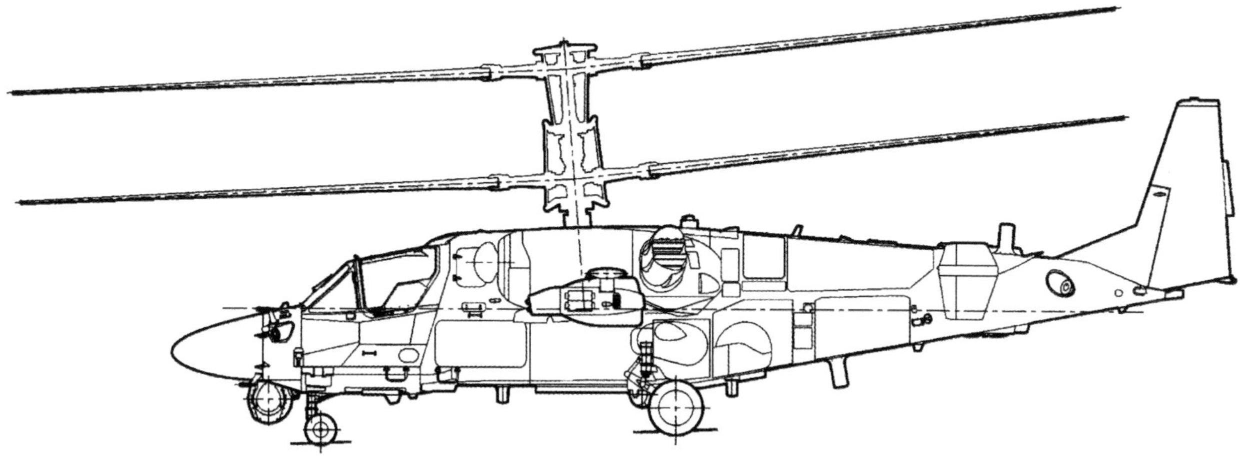

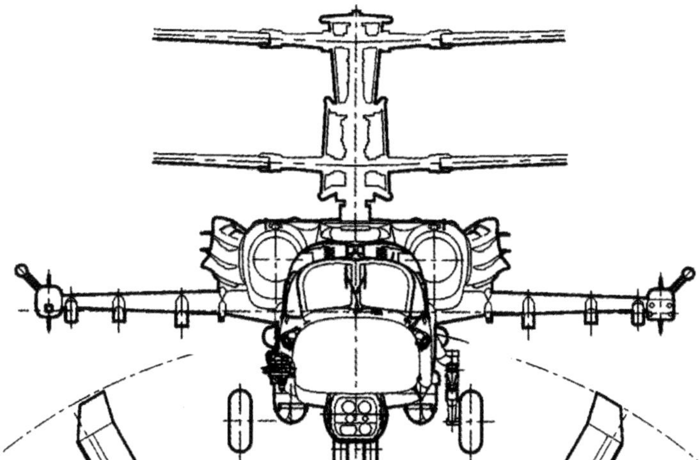

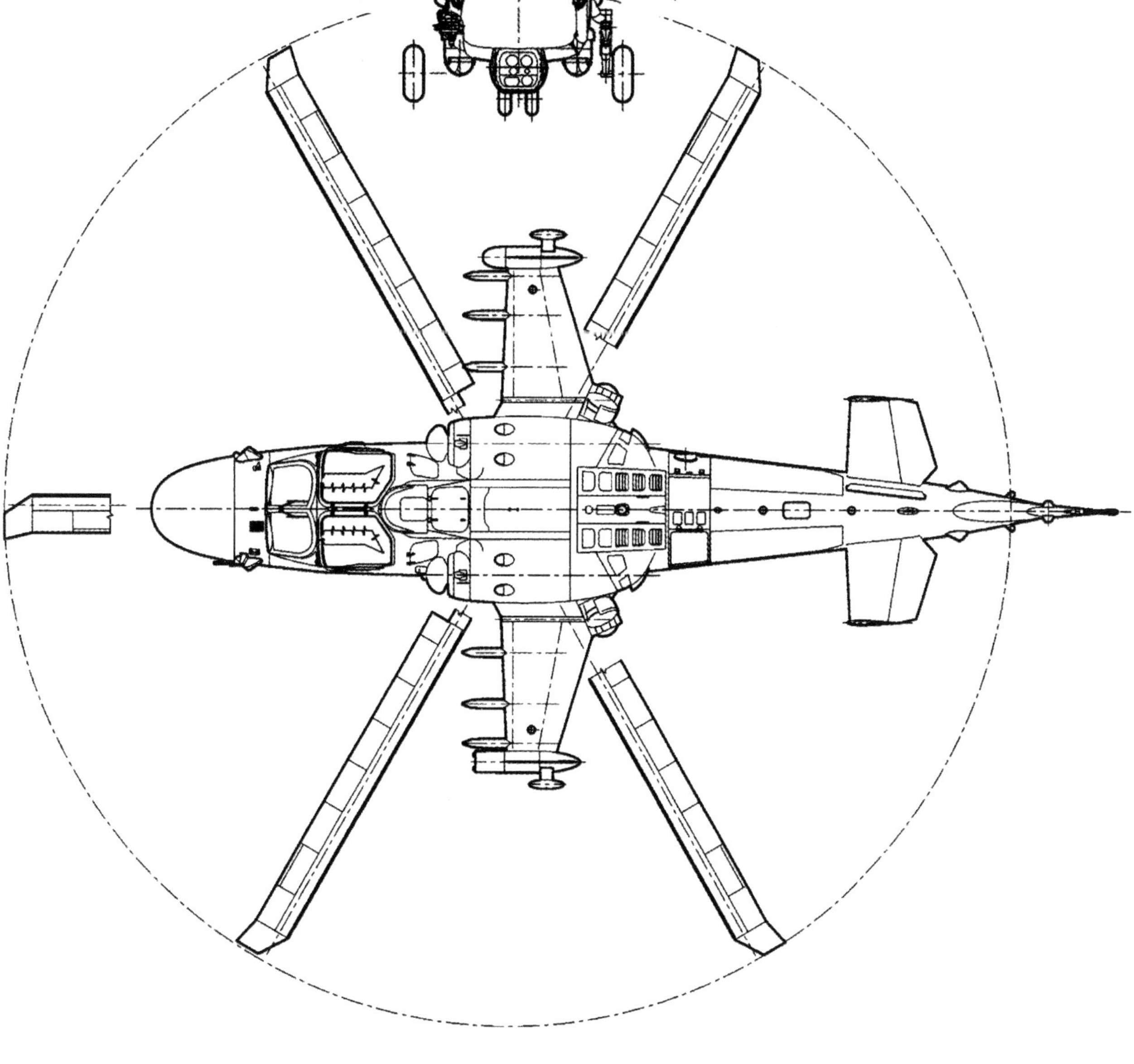

Three views of the production-standard Ka-52.

The Modeller's Corner

KAMOV **Ka-50** 1:72nd, 1:48th and 1:144th scale

Above: The box top of Esci's Ka-50 kit featuring the wrong designation.

So far the *Hokum* has received pretty extensive coverage – especially in **1:72nd scale.** **ESCI** (Ref. No. 9073, was the first to release a kit of the **Ka-50** in 1988, but this was wildly inaccurate; they even got the designation wrong as the 'Ka-34'! ESCI's kit was reissued in 1992 (they changed only the box, removing the designation but leaving the artist's impression); **AMT/ERTL** ran a rebox of ESCI issued in 1989 (Ref. No. 8852). The Chinese company **Dragon Models (DML)** also released a Ka-50 kit (Ref. No. 2509), which was copied by **HobbyBoss** (Ref. No. 87217); this kit was no good either. **Italeri** (Ref. No. 031) was the first to come up with a decent kit of the Ka-50 in 1994. This has also been marketed under other brands – **Tamiya** (Ref. No. 60718), **Revell** (Ref. No. 04406, both released in 1994), **Bilek** (Ref. No. 26), **C. C. Lee** (Ref. No. 00107), and **Zvezda** (Ref. No. 7216) and **Modelist** (Ref. No. 3519).

While the Italeri Ka-50 kit was generally acceptable, Zvezda decided to make a new and more accurate kit, using new moulds for the forward fuselage section, the wings and the rotor blades (the latter were too narrow in the old kit). Confusingly, it is listed under the same reference number 7216. The box art was also unchanged at first, so you had to look for the absence of the inscription 'Licensed by Italeri') on the side of the box.

Right and below: The HobbyBoss 1:72nd scale Ka-50 built 'out of the box' by Igor' Skoorikhin.

The latter contains four black plastic sprues with 133 parts and one clear one with six parts. The landing gear can be modelled extended or retracted. The main instrument panel is a bit primitive, but the instrument panel shroud, HUD frame and side consoles are OK. The weapons include Ataka ATGMs and B-8V20 FFAR pods; the latter unfortunately have the wrong number of tubes.

The new edition served as the basis for a kit of the night-capable **Ka-50Sh Night Hunter** (*sic*; Ref. No. 7272). The kit comprises 140 parts in dark brown plastic and six clear ones. The mouldings are crisp, with finely engraved panel lines, while the outlines of hatch covers and the lines on the rotor blades are raised.

In **1:48th scale** there is one Ka-50 kit on the market – **Italeri** (Ref. No. 845), which was reboxed by **Revell** (Ref. No. 04445). The kit comprises 123 parts in black plastic and nine clear parts; the mouldings are crisp, with engraved panel lines, and the kit goes together well. The rotors can be made to rotate – in the same direction unfortunately. Cockpit detail is a bit basic and the instrument panel shroud is in two halves (integral with the fuselage halves) of different thickness, but aftermarket parts are available to remedy this. The decal sheet is for two of the prototypes coded '018 White' (camouflaged) and '024 White outline' (black overall).

Revell also has a Ka-50 kit in **1:144th scale** (Ref. No. 4034).

Above: The box top of Zvezda's 1:72nd scale Ka-50 kit.

Left and below: The Zvezda Ka-50 built 'out of the box' by a modeller with the internet alias Airwolf. The model is painted with Tamiya paints.

KAMOV **Ka-52** 1:72nd scale

Right: The box top of Italeri's 1:72nd scale Ka-52 kit.

As for the **Ka-52**, injection moulded kits are available in 1:72nd scale only. This time **Italeri** led the way, releasing a kit in 1999 (Ref. No. 005). It shows the prototype in its 1998 configuration – that is, painted flat black overall, coded '061 White outline' and fitted with the Samshit dorsal optoelectronic system turret, a mast-mounted radome, a small ventral optoelectronic system turret to starboard and the Rotor optoelectronic system in the nose. This kit was subsequently reboxed by **Tamiya** (Ref. No. 60761) and **Zvezda** (Ref. No. 7224?). It is based on Italeri's Ka-50 from which two-thirds of the parts were borrowed as-is. The box contains two grey plastic sprues and one clear one with a total of 91 parts; some of them are left over from the Ka-50 and will not be needed, but 30 parts are new. Even though the fuselage halves (less cockpit section) appear identical to the Ka-50 items, the moulds have been reworked – the panel lines are engraved, not raised.

About the same time **Amodel** issued a thoroughly reworked version of Italeri's Ka-52 kit (Ref. No. 7211). The Ukrainian kit consists of 156 parts and includes decals by Fresco with 100-plus items; it is more accurate in some respects, but the quality of the castings is worse, since Amodel makes use of its traditional 'short run' technology, and the decals are of inferior quality, requiring MicroSet as they have very little adhesive. The kit goes together well, but a bit of putty is needed here and there, and the instruction sheet is rather haphazard. Again, the model portrays the prototype in its 1998 guise. The kit includes a wider choice of weapons and a more comprehensive decal sheet than Italeri's version.

Again, Zvezda later released a new Ka-52 (likewise listed as Ref. No. 7224), which is considered the best kit of the *Hokum-B* so far. Unfortunately it, too, represents the Ka-52 prototype (in its original configuration) – there is as yet no kit of the production model. **Revell** also has a Ka-52 kit (Ref. No. 04483) which is reportedly... a rebox of the new Zvezda kit! The box contains four black plastic sprues and one clear one; the canopy is in three pieces and can be left open. The dorsal optoelectronic turret is unfortunately moulded integrally with the forward fuselage halves and is thus in two halves – definitely a bad idea when it comes to filling and sanding the seam.

Aftermarket items for the *Hokum* in **1:72nd scale** include a resin kit of cockpit parts for Italeri's Ka-50 by **NeOmega** (Ref. No. C12) and a similar set for Italeri's Ka-52 (Ref. No. C32). Unfortunately the latter kit is all but incompatible with Amodel's version of the Ka-52. **Pavla** has a resin kit of cockpit parts for Italeri's Ka-50 (Ref. No. C72005) and a separate K-37-800 ejection seat (Ref. No. C72020); **Ace** offers a photo-etched parts set for the Ka-50's cockpit, rotor heads and FFAR pods. In **1:48th scale**, **Heliborne** offers a PE cockpit parts set (Ref. No. HCO 48007) for Revell's Ka-50; so does **Eduard**, while **Armycast** has an exterior parts set in resin.

Below: The Zvezda Ka-52 built 'out of the box' by a modeller with the internet alias 'kok'. The NeOmega resin cockpit set was used, and the model is painted with Akan paints, Tamiya and Akan varnish.